Caribbean
Desserts

Tropical Treats from your Favourite Islands

**Dedicated to my husband, Cecil,
and to our grandchildren**

Dr. Betty "K"

**author of the best-selling
Caribbean Cuisine and *Vegetarian Cuisine***

Front Cover
Tropical Fruit Salad, page 23

Caribbean Desserts
by
Dr. Betty "K"

First Printing — March 2000

Copyright © 2000 by
Betty K Books & Food
3 — 1750 The Queensway
Suite 1305
Etobicoke, Ontario
M9C 5H5
E-mail: bettyk@idirect.com   Fax: (416) 283-9285

Canadian Cataloguing in Publication Data

K., Betty

   Caribbean desserts : tropical treats from your favourite islands
   Includes index.

   ISBN 1-894022-43-2

1. Desserts – Caribbean Area.   Cookery, Caribbean.
I. Title.

TX773.K15 2000   641.8'6'09729   C00-920066-5

Photography by:
Patricia Holdsworth, Patricia Holdsworth Photography
Regina, Saskatchewan

Glass bowl on cover by:
Gilles Payette, Verre coulé du Québec inc., Saint-Sébastien, Québec

Glass bowl, vase and goblets on pages 17 and 103 by:
Robert Held, Robert Held Art Glass, Vancouver, British Columbia

Page formatting and indexing by Iona Glabus

Designed, Printed and Produced in Canada by:
Centax Books, a Division of PW Group
Publishing Director, Photo Designer & Food Stylist: Margo Embury
1150 Eighth Avenue, Regina, Saskatchewan, Canada S4R 1C9
(306) 525-2304   FAX (306) 757-2439
E-mail: centax@printwest.com   www.centaxbooks.com

Table of Contents

Recipes have been tested in U.S. Standard measurements. Common metric measurements are given as a convenience for those who are more familiar with metric. Recipes have not been tested in metric.

From the Author

Years of entertaining relatives and friends, in many parts of the world, inspired me to write my first book, **Caribbean Cuisine**. The enthusiasm of my readers and requests for vegetarian recipes inspired my second book, **Vegetarian Cuisine**. This third book, **Caribbean Desserts**, explores the luscious variety of island desserts.

I was born in Georgetown, Guyana, a former British Colony located on the northern coast of South America. I pursued undergraduate studies at McGill University, Montreal, then went on to study Medicine at the Royal College of Surgeons in Dublin, Ireland. I have lived and practised in Ireland, England, Trinidad, Guyana and Canada. I lived in Toronto for 7 years, then in the province of Saskatchewan for 12 years, where I started my first book, before returning to Toronto.

During my years as a student and a physician I have travelled many times to the Caribbean and have collected recipes from the islands I visited. Some of my Guyanese recipes were given to me by my mother, who helped me to expand my culinary skills. Indeed, we in the Caribbean are very proud of our cuisine and we take great delight in preparing and presenting our meals.

The recipes in this book explore the exotic flavours of the islands and take you on an international tour of many cultures.

Most of the ingredients are available at large North American supermarkets, and others are available at Oriental and West Indian grocery stores. I hope that you enjoy this taste of the Caribbean and take pleasure in sharing it with family and friends.

Introduction

Caribbean sunshine, tropical breezes, the turquoise sea, you can't take them home with you, but you can enjoy the flavours of the Caribbean forever. One of the highlights of your island holiday is the food, the amazing variety of island specialties. The world lives in the Caribbean. Lured by the climate and the riches of the new world, Europeans, Africans, Chinese and Indian settlers made the Caribbean their home. Every culture brought their culinary masterpieces and adapted and refined them in this tropical paradise.

Caribbean Cuisine and *Vegetarian Cuisine, Caribbean Style*, by Dr. Betty "K", have gained international recognition. Acclaimed by islanders and tourists, these traditional recipes retain the essential flavours of the originals, but have been adapted to the busy lifestyle of the author and contemporary cooks.

Caribbean Desserts is an exceptional collection of tropical treats. Succulent mango, refreshing lime, creamy coconut, fragrant guava, tangy pineapple, tart/sweet papaya, spicy ginger, the flavours of Caribbean desserts range from light and delicate to rich and decadent. Sweet and Fruit Breads include Mango Nut Bread with Mango Sauce and Spicy Gingerbread with Vanilla Custard Sauce. Other desserts include Mango Cake, Lime Daiquiri Pie, Mango, Soursop and Papaw ice creams, Mango Mousse and Orange Fluff, plus Gulab Jamoon, Rasmalai, Kheer and Peera. Tropical drinks, the perfect complement, round out these recipes – Piña Colada, Rum Punch, Ginger Beer, Mauby and Mango Wine.

Acknowledgements

I would like to thank my mother, Mrs. R. Kissoon, and my friends, Margo Embury, Diane Maynard and Patricia Fungon for their contribution of recipes for this book.

My thanks to my husband, Cecil, for his encouragement and contribution of the Caribbean proverbs, with help from Dyal Singh, Andy Singh and Colin Stephenson

Finally, my heartfelt thanks to Margo for all of her suggestions and her search for a hibiscus.

Map of the Caribbean

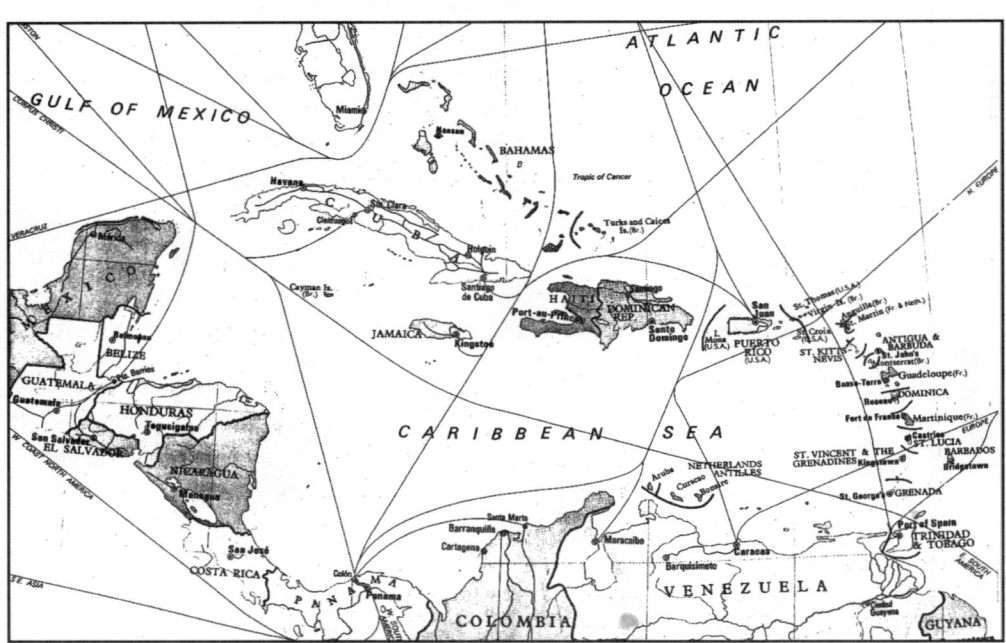

6

Tropical Drinks

Spiced Sorrel Drink

Sorrel has a tart flavour. This spicy drink is a favourite in Guyana and Trinidad.

4 cups	dried sorrel	1 L
1 tsp.	ground ginger	5 mL
1 tsp.	ground cinnamon	5 mL
3-4	whole cloves	3-4
	piece of dried orange peel	
1 tsp.	uncooked rice	5 mL
8 cups	cold water	2 L
4 cups	sugar or to taste	1 L

1. Cut red sepals from sorrel and sun-dry for 3 days.
2. Place dried sorrel in a jar with ginger, cinnamon, a few cloves, orange peel and rice.
3. Add cold water. Cover loosely; let stand at room temperature for 3 days.
4. Strain. Add sugar to taste. Chill and serve.

Yields about 2 quarts (2 L)

Variation: *Add rum to individual drinks if you want a Spicy Rum Cooler.*

Mauby

Mauby is a popular island drink. The bark comes from the carob tree.

1 tbsp.	dried mauby bark	15 mL
	small piece of ginger	
	piece of dried orange peel	
2	pieces of cinnamon stick	2
3-4	cloves	3-4
6 cups	cold water	1.5 L
2 cups	sugar	500 mL

1. Boil mauby bark, ginger, orange peel, cinnamon stick and cloves in 1 cup (250 mL) of water until flavour is strong – about 10 minutes.
2. Cool. Add water and sugar to taste. Strain.
3. Mauby may be served immediately, or bottle and refrigerate for about 2 days before serving ice cold. It will keep for 1-2 weeks.

Yields about 1½ quarts (1.5 L)

Ginger Beer

This popular Christmas drink has variations throughout the islands. It is refreshing year round.

8 oz.	ginger root	250 g
8 cups	water	2 L
1	lemon, juice of	1
4-5	cloves	4-5
4 cups	sugar	1 L
1 tbsp.	uncooked rice	15 mL

1. Grate the ginger. Combine ginger with water until desired strength is reached.
2. Add the juice of a lemon. Let stand for 20 minutes. Add cloves.
3. Add sugar to sweeten to taste.
4. Pour Ginger Beer into a large jar. Add rice. Cover and let stand for 2 days at room temperature.
5. Strain the beer through a thin muslin. Bottle in beer-type bottles and seal with corks OR put in refrigerator containers, cover and chill. Store, covered, overnight at room temperature. Refrigerate the next day. It will keep for up to 2 weeks.
6. Serve with crushed ice.

Guava Drink

Guava is a fragrant, sweet tropical fruit. Ripen green guavas at room temperature.

4 cups	ripe guavas	1 L
2 cups	sugar	500 mL
4 cups	water	1 L
	lemon slices	

1. Cut guavas in quarters and remove seeds.
2. Mash guava pulp and pass through a sieve.
3. Add sugar and water to pulp and mix well.
4. Chill the guava mixture before serving. Serve cold with lemon slices.

See photograph on page 17.

Soursop Punch

Soursop has a tart, acid flavour. It is part of the cherimoya, (custard apple) family, and is sometimes called sherbet fruit because the flavour is like a combination of mango, pineapple and strawberry.

1	soursop	1
	water	
2 cups	milk	500 mL
1 tsp.	vanilla	5 mL
1 cup	sugar	250 mL
1 cup	crushed ice	250 mL

1. Wash and peel the soursop. Remove the seeds.
2. Crush the pulp in a bowl. Add enough water to extract 3 cups (750 mL) of juice when you press the pulp through a sieve.
3. Add milk, vanilla and sugar to taste. Stir well. Refrigerate until serving.
4. Add crushed ice to serve.

Yields 5 cups (1.25 L)

Papaw Drink

Ripe papaya, or papaw or pawpaw, has a rich sweet/tart flavour.

1	ripe medium papaw (papaya)	1
4 cups	water	1 L
2 cups	evaporated milk	500 mL
	sugar to taste	
few drops	angostura bitters	few drops
	crushed ice	

1. Wash, peel and cut the papaw in half. Remove the seeds.
2. Crush the pulp thoroughly with a food masher.
3. Add water, milk, sugar, bitters and crushed ice.
4. Swizzle, strain and serve immediately over ice.

Yields 1½ quarts (1.5 L)

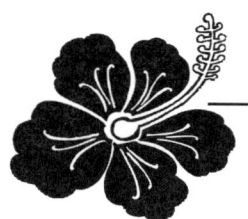

Mangoade

The rich luscious flavour of mango is even better with the addition of this tangy citrus mixture.

2 cups	chopped ripe mango	500 mL
¼ cup	sugar	60 mL
1½ cups	water	125 mL
1 tsp.	grated orange peel	5 mL
1½ cups	orange juice	375 mL
½ cup	lime juice	125 mL

1. Rub the mango pulp through a sieve.
2. Heat sugar, water and orange peel until sugar is dissolved.
3. Cool the sugar water mixture. Add the mango purée and fruit juices. Refrigerate until serving.
4. Serve cold over ice.

See photograph on page 51.

Golden Apple Drink

Golden apples (June Plums) are a tropical fruit with juicy tangy yellow flesh and one large prickly seed.

6	ripe golden apples*	6
4 cups	water	1 L
2 cups	sugar	500 mL
½ tsp.	almond extract	2 mL

1. Wash and peel golden apples. Grate or cut into small pieces.
2. Add water to the grated pulp and seeds.
3. Add sugar and almond extract. Stir until sugar is dissolved.
4. Strain the juice and refrigerate. Serve cold.

* Substitute tart yellow plums or Granny Smith Apples if Golden Apples are not available.

Tropical Fruit Punch

The sweet richness of pineapple has a triple citrus flavour boost.

2 cups	pineapple juice	500 mL
2 cups	grapefruit juice	500 mL
2 cups	orange juice	500 mL
¼ cup	lemon juice	60 mL
⅓ cup	honey	75 mL
3 x 12⅔ oz.	cans ginger ale	3 x 355 mL
1½ cups	chopped fruit – pineapple, mango, orange, etc.	375 mL

1. Combine all of the juices.
2. Sweeten to taste with honey. Chill for about 3 hours.
3. Pour the juice mixture into a punch bowl; stir in the ginger ale. Add the fruit. Serve over crushed ice.

Yields 2 quarts (2.5 L)

See photograph on page 103.

Rum Punch

I make my punch from a formula from England, 1-sour, 2-sweet, 3-strong, 4-weak.

1 oz.	lime juice	30 mL
2 oz.	prepared sugar syrup	60 mL
3 oz.	rum of choice	90 mL
4 oz.	iced water	113 mL
dash	angostura bitters	dash
	lemon slice for garnish	

1. Combine lime juice, syrup, rum and water; stir well. Chill.
2. Pour into a tall glass; add a few drops of angostura bitters. Garnish with a lemon slice.

Planter's Punch

Planter's Punch recipes vary from island to island. Some use dark rum, some use light and some use vodka or whiskey.

1 cup	lime juice	250 mL
1 cup	prepared sugar syrup*	250 mL
12 oz.	rum, vodka OR whiskey	341 mL
dash	angostura bitters	dash
2 cups	crushed ice	500 mL
1	banana	1
1	orange	1
	mint sprigs	

1. Blend lime juice, syrup, rum, bitters and ice in a blender at medium speed.
2. Serve in punch glasses and decorate with banana slices, orange pieces and mint sprigs.

* To make a **Simple Sugar Syrup**, combine 2 cups (500 mL) of sugar and 1 cup (250 mL) of water in a saucepan. Bring to a boil and boil for 5 minutes. Cool; refrigerate and use as needed.

Mango Wine

Green mangoes have a sharp tart/sweet refreshing flavour.

6	large green mangoes	6
6 cups	water	1.5 L
6 cups	sugar	1.5 L
3-4	cloves	3-4

1. Wash mangoes, peel and grate them.
2. Place the water in a jar; stir in sugar to dissolve; add grated fruit. Sprinkle in the cloves; leave covered for 10 days at room temperature.
3. Strain and bottle the wine. Seal the bottles with corks. Store for up to 2 weeks in the refrigerator.

Yields about 2 quarts (2 L)

Banana Liqueur

This liqueur has a rich mellow flavour.

1 cup	rum	250 mL
1 cup	crushed ripe bananas	250 mL
1 lb.	sugar	500 g
4 cups	water	1 L
1 cup	brandy	250 mL

1. Pour rum over crushed banana. Let stand for 1 week at room temperature.
2. Boil sugar and water for 15 minutes. Pour over banana mixture. Add brandy.
3. Strain and bottle. This liqueur is ready to drink immediately and may be stored, refrigerated, for up to 3-4 weeks.

Yields about 1½ quarts (1.5 L)

Banana Daiquiri

Creamy and smooth, this is a pleasure on a hot day, or when you're dreaming of the tropics.

¼ cup	light rum	60 mL
1 tsp.	banana liqueur, above	5 mL
1 tsp.	lime juice	5 mL
½	small banana, chopped	½
½ cup	crushed ice	125 mL

1. Combine all ingredients in a blender. Blend until smooth and frothy.

Serves 1

Piña Colada

Coconut and pineapple are the ultimate tropic combination. This version uses the lighter coconut milk, rather than coconut cream.

1½ cups	coconut milk	375 mL
1½ cups	pineapple juice	375 mL
½ cup	pineapple tidbits	125 mL
13½ oz.	evaporated milk	385 mL
¼ cup	light rum	60 mL
	crushed ice	
	pineapple slices for garnish	

1. Combine coconut milk, pineapple juice, pineapple tidbits, evaporated milk and rum. Blend until smooth.
2. Add ice. Blend until creamy.
3. Pour into tall glasses. Decorate each glass with a pineapple slice.

Ponche De Crème

A creamy Caribbean version of eggnog.

6	eggs	6
	piece of lemon peel	
3 x 13½ oz.	cans evaporated milk	3 x 385 mL
10 oz.	can condensed milk	300 mL
1 tsp.	angostura bitters	5 mL
1 tsp.	grated nutmeg	5 mL
½ cup	rum	125 mL
	crushed ice	

1. Beat eggs with the lemon peel until light.
2. Add evaporated milk, condensed milk, bitters, nutmeg and rum. Beat lightly.
3. Remove lemon peel. Serve over crushed ice.

Serves 8

Creole Eggnog

This recipe was given to me by a friend from Trinidad. It is a rich and luxurious eggnog, with a hint of lemon.

6	eggs	6
2 x 10 oz.	cans condensed milk	2 x 300 g
1	lemon, grated peel of	1
1 tsp.	vanilla	5 mL
few drops	angostura bitters	few drops
1 cup	rum	250 mL

1. Beat eggs well in a large bowl. Add milk, grated peel, vanilla and bitters, mixing well.
2. Stir in rum and serve over crushed ice.

Serves 4-6

Banana Pineapple Eggnog

This delicious eggnog has no rum but lots of flavour.

1	ripe banana	1
1	egg, beaten	1
1 cup	cold milk	250 mL
1 tsp.	sugar	5 mL
½ tsp.	vanilla	2 mL
2 tbsp.	pineapple juice	30 mL

1. Crush the banana with a fork. Beat until creamy.
2. Mix the beaten egg with milk; add puréed banana.
3. Add sugar, vanilla and pineapple juice. Mix thoroughly.
4. Chill and serve.

Serves 1-2

Caribbean
Fresh Fruit Desserts

Ginger Mango Sauce

Ginger adds snap to the rich mango flavour – serve over ice cream or pound cake.

3 cups	finely chopped very ripe mango (3 mangoes)	750 mL
2 tbsp.	sugar or more to taste	30 mL
¼ cup	minced candied ginger in syrup* OR crystallized ginger	60 mL
2 tsp.	fresh lime juice	10 mL

1. Combine 2 cups chopped mango and sugar in a food processor. Pureé until smooth. In a medium bowl, combine pureé and remaining chopped mango. Stir in ginger and lime juice.
2. Let stand for 1 hour up to overnight. Cover and refrigerate if keeping longer than 1-2 hours.

Yields 3 cups (750 mL)

* If using candied ginger, add 1 tbsp. (15 mL) of the syrup, or more to taste.

Caribbean Fruit Frappé

This is a creamy refreshing light dessert or drink.

2 cups	chopped pineapple	500 mL
2 cups	frozen vanilla yogurt	500 mL
2 cups	chopped mango	500 mL
3 tbsp.	lime juice	45 mL
1 tsp.	vanilla OR rum extract OR 3 tbsp. (45 mL) rum	5 mL

1. Place all ingredients in a blender and blend until smooth.

Serves 4

Chilled Pineapple & Papaya

Serve this refreshing soup as a light dessert as an appetizer or even as a drink.

2 cups	chopped pineapple	500 mL
³/₄ cup	chopped cantaloupe	175 mL
1 cup	chopped ripe papaya	250 mL
1 cup	unsweetened apricot or mango nectar	250 mL
³/₄ cup	soda water or ginger ale	175 mL
1 tbsp.	chopped fresh mint leaves mint sprigs for garnish	15 mL

1. Place all fruit in a food processor and purée.
2. Stir in juice, soda water and chopped mint.
3. Refrigerate, covered, until well chilled, for 3-4 hours.
4. Serve in bowls or wine glasses and garnish with mint sprigs.

Serves 2-3

Bucket a go well every day, one day de bottom must fall out.

If you lie every day, one day the truth will be known.

Caribbean Fruit Kebabs with Creamy Lime Sauce

This makes a refreshing light dessert.

CREAMY LIME SAUCE:

1 cup	sour cream OR yogurt*	250 mL
2 tbsp.	fresh lime juice	30 mL
2 tbsp.	sugar	30 mL
1½ tsp.	grated lime peel	7 mL
1	ripe papaya, peeled, halved, seeded**	1
1	small ripe pineapple, peeled, cored	1
2	large bananas, peeled	2
1 tbsp.	lime juice	15 mL
8 x 12"	bamboo skewers	8 x 30 cm

1. To make the sauce, combine sour cream, lime juice, sugar and lime peel in small bowl. Cover and refrigerate.
2. Cut papaya and pineapple into 24, 1" (2.5 cm) pieces each. Cut bananas into 1" (2.5 cm) chunks. Toss bananas with lime juice.
3. Alternate the fruit on the skewers. (Arrange on a platter up to 1 hour before serving. Cover and chill.)
4. Serve with Creamy Lime Sauce.

Serves 6-8

* Use low-fat sour cream or yogurt if you prefer.

** Save papaya seeds to add peppery flavour to creamy salad dressings. Just whirl the seeds, in a blender or food processor, into prepared ranch or creamy cucumber dressings.

Tropical Fruit Salad

The colours and fresh flavours of this salad take you back to the islands.

1 cup	cubed pineapple	250 mL
1 cup	orange segments	250 mL
1 cup	grapefruit segments	250 mL
1 cup	cubed papaw (papaya)	250 mL
1 cup	sliced mango	250 mL
1 cup	cubed melon	250 mL
¼ cup	honey	60 mL
½ cup	orange juice	125 mL
1 cup	sliced bananas	250 mL
¼ cup	chopped nuts of your choice, almonds, macadamia nuts, etc. (optional)	60 mL

1. Combine all fruits, except bananas, in a large glass bowl.
2. Dissolve honey in orange juice. Pour over the fruit and chill.
3. Just before serving add sliced bananas and chopped nuts. Serve with ice cream or whipped cream.

Variation: *For a spectacular presentation, garnish with thinly sliced carambola (star fruit) and star anise or dried pomegranate seeds (anardana).*

Pictured on the front cover.

oon arun till day ketcham.

One day you will be caught for your wrongdoing.

Citrus-Ginger Fruit Salad

A refreshing explosion of flavours.

1 tb⸴p.	minced fresh ginger	15 mL
1	orange, juice of	1
1	lime, juice of	1
1	lemon, juice of	1
2	large mangoes, diced	2
1	small pineapple, diced	1
2	very ripe papayas, diced	2
	sugar to taste	
2 cups	raspberries	500 mL

1. In a large glass bowl, combine ginger and juices. Add all of the fruit, except the raspberries. Add sugar; toss lightly; chill for 2-3 hours.
2. Gently stir in raspberries just before serving.

Serves 8

Mango Berry Parfait

1	mango, peeled, cubed	1
2 tbsp.	orange juice	30 mL
¼ cup	vanilla, lemon or plain yogurt	60 mL
2 cups	sliced strawberries OR 1 cup (250 mL) sliced strawberries and 1 cup (250 mL) raspberries	50 mL
2	kiwis, peeled, sliced	2
	mint sprigs for garnish	

1. In a blender or processor, combine the mango, orange juice and yogurt. Purée and chill until ready to serve.
2. In champagne or parfait glasses, layer mango purée, berries and kiwi.
3. Garnish with whole berries and mint sprigs.

Serves 2-3

Tropical Fruit with Mango or Pineapple Sorbet

Only a fruit sorbet could make fresh fruit taste even better.

SUGAR-WINE SYRUP:

³/₄ cup	water	175 mL
¹/₂ cup	dry white wine	125 mL
¹/₂ cup	sugar	125 mL
2 cups	cubed pineapple	500 mL
3	kiwis, peeled, sliced	3
2 cups	cubed mango	500 mL
2 tbsp.	fresh lime juice	30 mL
1 tsp.	grated lime peel	15 mL
3 cups	mango or pineapple sorbet	750 mL

1. In a small saucepan, combine water, wine and sugar. Bring to a boil and stir until sugar dissolves. Chill sugar-wine syrup until cold.
2. Combine fruit, lime juice, peel and chilled syrup in a large glass bowl. Cover and refrigerate for 1 hour or overnight.
3. In 6 individual serving dishes or wineglasses, layer chilled fruit and sorbet.

Serves 6

Waan waan dutty bill dam.

Saving pennies daily, will eventually bring you wealth.

Pineapple & Kiwi with Mango Rum Sauce

Try this great sauce over ice cream or a plain pound cake.

MANGO RUM SAUCE:

2	very ripe mangoes, peeled, chopped	2
	dark rum to taste	
	sugar to taste	
6	kiwis, peeled, sliced	6
1	fresh pineapple, cut into small spears	1
	mint sprigs for garnish	

1. To make Mango Rum Sauce, in a blender or processor, purée the mango. Add rum and sugar to taste.
2. In shallow bowls, arrange kiwi and pineapple. Spoon Mango Rum Sauce over the fruit. Garnish with mint and serve.

Serves 4-5

Papaw Delight

1	medium ripe papaw (papaya)	1
4 tbsp.	butter OR margarine	60 mL
1 tbsp.	flour	15 mL
1 cup	milk	250 mL
½ cup	sugar	125 mL
1 tsp.	vanilla	5 mL

1. Wash, peel and slice papaw, removing seeds.
2. Melt butter and stir in flour. Stir in milk a little at a time. Bring to a boil. Add sugar and vanilla.
3. Place sliced papaw in a greased 8" (20 cm) ovenproof dish. Pour milk mixture over papaw.
4. Bake at 350°F (180°C) for about 45 minutes, or until golden brown.

Papaw Delight

(Continued)

Variation: *To give this tropical fruit dish a North American twist, make it into a **Papaw Crisp** with a crunchy oatmeal, brown sugar topping. Combine ½ cup (125 mL) each of flour, rolled oats, and brown sugar with ¼ cup (60 mL) of melted butter and a dash of nutmeg. Mix until crumbly and sprinkle over papaw slices before baking.*

Caramelized Mango Cream

Crunchy brown sugar topping over whipped cream and tropical fruit.

1½ cups	**chopped mango**	375 mL
1 cup	**chopped papaya**	250 mL
½ cup	**fresh raspberries (optional)**	125 mL
	white sugar to taste	
2 cups	**whipping cream**	500 mL
	brown sugar for topping	

1. Place the fruit in a shallow 8-10" (20-25 cm) baking dish. Sprinkle with a bit of sugar and stir gently.
2. Beat cream until thick. Spread cream evenly over the fruit. Cover fruit completely with cream, sealing all edges of the dish.
3. Chill in the refrigerator for 1-2 hours or place in the freezer for 20-30 minutes.
4. Sprinkle cream with enough brown sugar to make a thin, even layer, about ¼" (1 cm) thick.
5. Place the baking dish on a cookie sheet. Preheat broiler to red hot. Broil dessert until sugar melts and caramelizes. Watch carefully – do not burn.
6. Chill in refrigerator until serving time.

Serves 4-6

Variation: *Sprinkle 2 tbsp. (30 mL) minced fresh, crystallized or candied ginger over the fruit before topping with whipped cream.*

Bananas with Rum Raisin Sauce

These flavours belong together, rich, smooth and delicious.

½ cup	raisins	125 mL
3 tbsp.	rum	45 mL

RUM SAUCE:

½ cup	butter	125 mL
¼ cup	water	60 mL
¼ cup	rum	60 mL
1 tbsp.	lemon juice	15 mL
1	lemon, grated peel of	1
1 tsp.	vanilla OR 2 tbsp. (30 mL) banana liqueur	5 mL
6	small bananas	6
6 scoops	vanilla ice cream	6 scoops

1. In a small bowl, combine raisins and 3 tbsp. (45 mL) rum. Let stand at room temperature for ½ to 1 hour.
2. In a heavy frying pan, melt butter and add water. Cook until reduced and thickened to a heavy syrup.
3. Add rum, lemon juice and peel and vanilla.
4. Peel bananas and halve lengthwise. Cut halves in half (24 pieces in total).
5. Place bananas in hot rum sauce; add rum-soaked raisins and heat through.
6. Place the ice cream in individual bowls. Top each with 4 banana pieces, raisins and sauce. Serve immediately.

Serves 6

Variations: *For **Caramelized Bananas**, add 2 cups (500 mL) packed brown sugar to butter in frying pan. If you wish add 1 tsp. (5 mL) cinnamon.*

Caramelized Papaya Strips

Succulent papaya strips in a caramel cinnamon sauce – perfect for serving over ice creams or with Ginger Pound Cake, page 89, and whipped cream.

2 cups	sugar	500 mL
2	small cinnamon sticks	2
3	small firm papayas (peeled, seeded, cut lengthwise in ½" (1.3 cm) strips	3

1. In a large heavy saucepan, spread ⅔ cup (150 mL) sugar, add the cinnamon sticks, and top with half of the papaya strips. Sprinkle another ⅔ cup (150 mL) sugar on top, add the remaining papaya strips; top with the remaining ⅔ cup (150 mL) of sugar.
2. Cook, covered, over moderately low heat. Shake the pan occasionally (do not stir), for 35 to 45 minutes, until the sugar is dissolved completely.
3. Simmer the papaya strips, uncovered, for 10 minutes, until they become translucent.
4. Cool, cover and refrigerate. Keeps up to 1 month.

Yields about 1 quart (1 L)

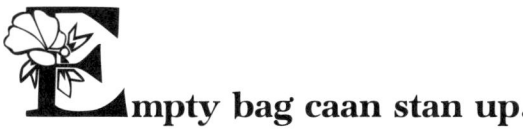

Empty bag caan stan up.

Without food you cannot work.

Strawberry Mango Meringues

Crisp meringues make a light and lovely dessert with your choice of fresh fruit. With sorbet instead of whipped cream, it's also low fat!

4	**egg whites, room temperature**	4
1 tsp.	**vanilla**	5 mL
⅛ tsp.	**cream of tartar**	0.5 mL
1 cup	**sugar, less 1 tbsp. (15 mL)**	220 mL
2 cups	**sliced strawberries**	500 mL
2	**medium mangoes, peeled, diced**	2
1 tbsp.	**brown sugar**	15 mL
2 tbsp.	**rum**	30 mL
½ cup	**whipping cream**	125 mL
1 tbsp.	**sugar**	15 mL
1 tsp.	**vanilla**	5 mL

1. Beat egg whites until foamy. Add vanilla and cream of tartar. Beat in sugar, 1 tbsp. (15 mL) at a time, until meringue holds stiff peaks.
2. Preheat oven to 225°F (107°C). Line 2 baking sheets with parchment paper.
3. With 2 large spoons, shape the meringue paste into 8 individual nests, 4 on each baking sheet.
4. Place the pans in the oven and bake for about 1 hour. Meringue should be thoroughly dry but not coloured. Turn off the heat and allow meringues to cool in the oven.
5. Combine strawberries, mangoes, brown sugar and rum. Set aside until ready to serve.
6. To serve, whip cream with sugar until soft peaks form. Add vanilla. Place a dab of whipped cream in the bottom of each meringue shell. Spoon in fruit mixture, dividing evenly. Top with another dollop of whipped cream and serve.

Serves 8

Variation: *Substitute lemon or mango sorbet or vanilla ice cream for the whipped cream in the meringue shells and top with the fruit.*

See photograph on page 17.

30

Frozen Sorbet & Fruit Flan

Beautiful, colourful and full of flavour, enjoy the textures in this tropical dessert.

GINGERSNAP BROWN SUGAR CRUST:

3 cups	gingersnap cookie crumbs	750 mL
½ cup	packed brown sugar	125 mL
2 tsp.	ground ginger	10 mL
¾ cup	melted unsalted butter	175 mL
4 cups	mango sorbet, slightly softened	1 L
2 cups	lemon or lime sorbet, slightly softened	500 mL
2 cups	chopped fresh pineapple	500 mL
1	papaya, peeled, seeded, chopped	1
1	mango, peeled, pitted, chopped	1
2 cups	sliced strawberries OR blueberries OR raspberries OR a combination	500 mL
	toasted shredded sweetened coconut (optional)	

1. To make the crust, combine crumbs, brown sugar and ginger in a large bowl. Stir in melted butter. Press over bottom and up sides of a 9" (23 cm) springform pan. Freeze until firm, about 30 minutes.
2. Spread mango sorbet over crust; freeze until firm, about 20 minutes. Spread lemon sorbet over mango sorbet. Freeze until firm, about 30 minutes. Keep frozen until ready to serve. It will keep for 1-2 days.
3. Combine all fruit.
4. Remove filled crust from springform pan. Place on a platter and spoon fruit over sorbet. Sprinkle with coconut, if using, and serve.

Serves 8

Tropical Sundae with Ginger Lime Sauce

Warm Ginger Lime Sauce adds punch to ice cream and tropical fruit.

GINGER LIME SAUCE:

½ cup	white sugar	125 mL
½ cup	packed brown sugar	125 mL
6 tbsp.	water	90 mL
¼ cup	fresh lime juice	60 mL
3 tbsp.	butter	45 mL
1-2	pieces crystallized ginger	1-2
3 tbsp.	minced crystallized ginger	45 mL
4-6 cups	vanilla OR mango ice cream	1-1.5 L
3 cups	diced fruit (pineapple, papaya and/or mango)	750 mL
	toasted sweetened shredded coconut (optional)	

1. To make the sauce, combine the sugars, water, juice, butter and first amount of ginger in a heavy medium saucepan. Stir over medium heat until sugars dissolve. Simmer until reduced to 1 cup (250 mL), stirring frequently, about 15 minutes. Cool to lukewarm. Discard ginger pieces and stir in minced ginger. Cover and store at room temperature for up to 1 day. Reheat to lukewarm before serving.
2. To make sundaes, place ice cream in 6 serving dishes. Spoon warm sauce over ice cream and top with fruit. Sprinkle with coconut, if using, and serve.

Serves 6

Caribbean Fruit Sundae with Fruit Rum Sauce

Smooth and rich, this caramelized fruit sauce is superb.

FRUIT RUM SAUCE:

½ cup	white sugar	125 mL
½ cup	firmly packed Demerara sugar	125 mL
⅓ cup	water	75 mL
¼ cup	frozen pineapple OR mango OR orange juice concentrate, thawed orange juice	60 mL
3 tbsp.	butter	45 mL
2 tbsp.	dark rum	30 mL
3-4 cups	mango, lemon OR strawberry frozen yogurt OR vanilla OR mango ice cream	750 mL-1 L
2 cups	chopped fruit (mango, papaya, banana and pineapple)	500 mL

1. To make the sauce, in a heavy saucepan over medium heat, combine the sugars, water, juice and butter. Heat and stir until sugar dissolves. Simmer until reduced to 1 cup (250 mL), about 10 minutes. Stir in rum. Cover and refrigerate for up to 2 days. Reheat to lukewarm before serving.
2. To make sundaes, spoon frozen yogurt or ice cream into 4 dishes. Spoon the Fruit Rum Sauce over yogurt or ice cream and top with fruit.

Serves 4

Pineapple Split with Mango Sauce

Refreshing sorbet and fresh pineapple with mango or papaya sauce.

1 cup	mango OR papaya juice	250 mL
½ cup	sugar	125 mL
3 cups	chopped fresh pineapple	750 mL
4 cups	mango OR pineapple sorbet	1 L
1 cup	toasted shredded sweetened coconut (optional)	250 mL
	mint sprigs	

1. In a heavy saucepan over high heat, stir mango juice and sugar until sugar dissolves and syrup comes to a boil. Boil until reduced to ⅔ cup (150 mL), about 5 minutes. Cool syrup. Cover and let stand at room temperature for up to 1 day.
2. To make sundaes, spoon sorbet into 6 dishes. Top with pineapple and Mango Sauce. Sprinkle with coconut if using. Garnish with mint sprigs.

Serves 6

Banana Splits with Sorbet

Sorbet replaces ice cream in this tropical treat.

2	ripe medium bananas, peeled and cut lengthwise, then cut crosswise into quarters (8 pieces in total)	2
2 cups	passion fruit OR mango sorbet	500 mL
1 cup	raspberry sorbet	250 mL
2	medium kiwis, peeled, sliced	2
¼ cup	toasted shredded coconut (optional)	60 mL

1. In each of 4 shallow bowls, place 2 banana quarters. Spoon sorbets between bananas. Top with kiwi and toasted coconut, if using.

Serves 4

Ice Creams & Sorbet

Ice Cream

With this basic custard you can make a delicious range of ice creams – look at the following recipes for ideas and then use your imagination.

BASIC CUSTARD FOR ICE CREAM:

4	eggs	4
½ cup	sugar	125 mL
1 tbsp.	custard powder	15 mL
3 cups	milk	750 mL
½ tsp.	vanilla	2 mL

1. Beat the eggs and sugar lightly.
2. Dissolve the custard powder in ¼ cup (60 mL) of milk; add to the remaining milk and beat well.
3. Stir the milk mixture into the egg mixture. Place in a double boiler over hot water; continue stirring until the custard mixture coats the spoon. Cool. Add vanilla. Use in ice cream recipes that follow.

Coconut Ice Cream

Creamy, smooth coconut ice cream – this is not easy to find commercially, now you can make your own.

COCONUT MILK:

2 cups	grated coconut OR dessicated coconut	500 mL
2 cups	hot water	500 mL

1. Soak coconut in hot water. Allow to rest until cool.
2. Place in a muslin bag and squeeze out the coconut milk.

FOR PREPARATION OF ICE CREAM:
1. Add **2 cups (500 mL) of coconut milk** to the **basic custard**, omitting the vanilla and replacing it with **almond extract**. Mix well.
2. Process in an ice-cream maker according to the manufacturers directions or place in a freezing tray and freeze until half frozen. Remove, beat well and return to the freezing compartment.

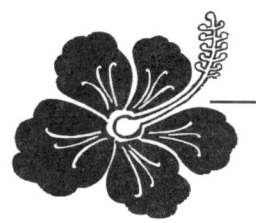

Mango Ice Cream

The flavour of mango is the essence of the tropics.

| 1 cup | mango pulp | 250 mL |
| ¼ cup | sugar | 60 mL |

1. Combine mango pulp with sugar.
2. Add **basic custard** from page 36 and mix thoroughly.
3. Freeze as in the preparation method for Coconut Ice Cream, page 36.

Soursop Ice Cream

Try this unique flavour, tart and refreshing.

| 1 | soursop, peeled, seeded | 1 |
| ½ cup | water | 125 mL |

1. To soursop, add water and blend in a food processor.
2. Add the **basic custard** page 36, omitting vanilla extract.
3. Freeze as in the preparation method for Coconut Ice Cream, page 36.

Han wash han mek han come clean.

If you help me today, someone will help you tomorrow.

Papaw Ice Cream

Very ripe papaws give the best flavour.

1 cup	mashed papaw (papaya)	250 mL
¼ cup	sugar	60 mL
1 tbsp.	lime juice	15 mL

1. Combine the papaw pulp, sugar and lime juice.
2. Add the **basic custard** page 36, omitting vanilla and mixing thoroughly.
3. Freeze as in the preparation method for Coconut Ice Cream, page 36.

Jamaican Ginger Ice Cream

Fast, easy and very good.

1 qt.	rich chocolate, coffee OR vanilla ice cream	1 L
4 tbsp.	finely chopped candied ginger in heavy syrup, or more to taste	60 mL

1. Soften ice cream and stir in ginger. Return ice cream to the freezer.
2. When serving ice cream, spoon a little of the ginger syrup over each serving.

Yields 1 quart (1 L)

Variations: *Minced candied ginger is also very good in Mango, Apricot, Peach or Pawpaw ice creams.*

Creamy Mango Ice Cream

Use very ripe mangoes for the most intense flavour.

¼ tsp.	cream of tartar	1 mL
8 oz.	berry (superfine) sugar (1 cup [250 mL])	250 g
4 tbsp.	water	60 mL
4	very ripe mangoes	4
1	lime, strained juice of	1
2 cups	whipping cream, lightly whipped	500 mL

1. Mix the cream of tartar and sugar with the water. Bring to a boil and cook over low heat, stirring until the syrup thickens. Let cool.
2. Peel, remove stones and sieve mangoes; the mangoes should yield about 1¼ cups (300 mL) of purée.
3. Add mango purée to syrup with lime juice. Stir in cream until well blended.
4. Process in an ice-cream maker according to the manufacturer's directions or turn into a freezing tray and freeze. When half-frozen, remove from freezer and beat well. Freeze until firm.

Serves 4-5

Variation: *For* **Apricot** *or* **Peach Ice Cream**, *ripe apricots or peaches can be used in exactly the same way as mangoes and lemon juice can take the place of lime.*

Black boulangey – mo you clean am mo e shine.

The more you practise your skills the better you will become.

39

Mango Ice Cream with Macadamia Nuts

Mangoes and macadamia nuts are perfect complements.

2 cups	whipping cream	500 mL
1 cup	whole milk	250 mL
6	egg yolks	6
1 cup	sugar	250 mL
2	large very ripe mangoes, diced	2
2 tsp.	fresh lime juice OR ¼ cup (60 mL) white rum	10 mL
½ tsp.	grated lime peel	2 mL
1 cup	toasted, coarsely chopped unsalted macadamia nuts	250 mL

1. Bring cream and milk to a boil in a heavy saucepan.
2. Whisk yolks and sugar together in a bowl. Gradually whisk hot cream into yolk mixture. Return to saucepan. Stir over low heat until custard thickens, about 5 minutes. Transfer custard to a blender or food processor. Add mangoes and blend until smooth.
3. Chill custard. Stir in juice, peel and nuts. Process in an ice-cream maker according to the manufacturer's instructions. Freeze ice cream in a covered container and keep for up to 2 days.

Yields about 5 cups (1.25 L)

ot a tell kettle e bottom black.

Before you criticize someone, you should think about your own faults.

Kulfi

This traditional East Indian ice cream has made itself at home in the Caribbean. The distinctive flavour can become addictive.

13½ oz.	can evaporated milk	385 mL
10 oz.	can condensed milk	300 mL
1 cup	whipping cream, whipped	250 mL
¼ tsp.	cardamom	1 mL
	few strands of saffron	
6	almonds, blanched, chopped	6
6	pistachios, unsalted, chopped	6

1. In a blender or food processor, blend all the above ingredients.
2. Pour into a shallow dish and place in the freezer to set.
3. Remove from the freezer about 15 minutes before serving.

o so na like so.

Don't do things to others that you would not like done to you.

Mango Daiquiri Sorbet

Rich fruit flavour with a rum punch!

1¼ cups	water	300 mL
¾ cup	sugar	175 mL
2 cups	chopped mango	500 mL
½ cup	white rum	125 mL
	fresh mango slices	

1. Combine water and sugar in a heavy saucepan over medium heat. Stir until sugar dissolves. Bring to a boil and add chopped mango. Return mixture to a boil for 1-2 minutes.
2. In a food processor, purée mango and liquid.
3. Refrigerate mango purée for 2-3 hours.
4. Stir rum into purée and process in an ice-cream mixer according to manufacturer's instructions. Store in a covered container in the freezer until firm, 2-3 hours, or keep for up to 2 days.
5. Garnish with fresh mango slices to serve.

Serves 4

Variation: *For **Raspberry Sorbet**, substitute 2 cups (500 mL) of fresh or frozen and thawed raspberries for the mango. Strain raspberry pulp and discard the seeds.*

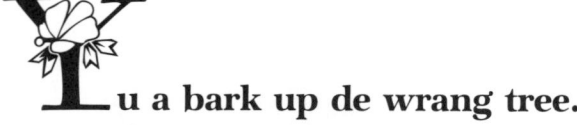

Yu a bark up de wrang tree.

You are asking the wrong person.

Mousses, Custards
&
Trifles

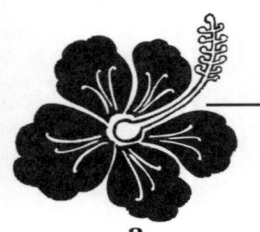

Mango Mousse

Rich but light, this is perfect after a heavy meal.

3	egg whites	3
¾ cup	sugar	175 mL
1 cup	mango pulp	250 mL
1 cup	whipping cream	250 mL
	mango slices for garnish	

1. Beat the egg whites until very stiff. Add sugar and continue to beat.
2. Fold in mango pulp.
3. Beat whipping cream; add to mango mixture.
4. Spoon mango mixture into individual glasses. Chill.
5. Garnish with mango slices before serving.

Serves 4

See photograph on page 51.

Mango Mousse with Yogurt

1 tbsp.	unflavoured gelatine (1 env.)	15 mL
¼ cup	cold water	60 mL
2	large very ripe mangoes	2
⅓ cup	sugar	75 mL
½ tsp.	vanilla	2 mL
1 cup	plain OR vanilla yogurt	250 mL
1 cup	whipping cream	250 mL
	mango slices for garnish	
	mint for garnish (optional)	

1. In a small saucepan, sprinkle gelatine over cold water and let soften for 1 minute. Heat over low heat until gelatine is dissolved.
2. In a food processor or blender, combine and pureé the mango, sugar and vanilla. Add the gelatine mixture and mix well. Transfer the mango mixture to a bowl and fold in the yogurt.
3. Beat cream until it holds stiff peaks. Gently fold into mango mixture.
4. Chill the mousse for 4 hours or overnight. Garnish individual servings with mango slices and mint.

Serves 4

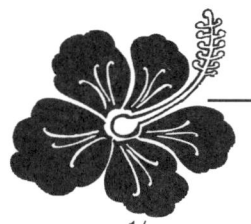

Mango Rum Mousse

Raspberries and a rich mango rum combo.

½ cup	fresh orange juice	125 mL
1 tbsp.	fresh lime juice	15 mL
2 tsp.	unflavoured gelatine	10 mL
1	large ripe mango, chopped	1
½ cup	sour cream* (may be light)	125 mL
½ cup	whole milk	125 mL
⅓ cup	sugar	75 mL
1½ tbsp.	light OR dark rum	22 mL
1 cup	fresh raspberries	250 mL

1. Combine juices in a small pan. Sprinkle gelatine over; let stand for 10 minutes. Stir over low heat until gelatine dissolves. Let cool but not set.
2. In a processor or blender, combine mango, sour cream, milk, sugar and rum. Blend until smooth. Blend in gelatine mixture.
3. Pour mousse into 6 dessert dishes or wine glasses. Cover and chill for 4 hours or overnight. Sprinkle with raspberries before serving.

Serves 6

Tropical Chocolate Mousse

¼ cup	sugar	60 mL
¼ cup	rum	60 mL
¼ tsp.	cinnamon (optional)	1 mL
4 oz.	sweet chocolate (4 squares)	125 g
2 tbsp.	whipping cream	30 mL
2	egg whites, stiffly beaten	2
1 cup	whipping cream, whipped	250 mL

1. In a heavy skillet, over low heat, cook sugar and rum just until sugar is dissolved but not caramelized or browned. Add cinnamon, if using.
2. Melt chocolate and stir in first amount of cream. Stir in rum mixture and let cool.
3. Fold beaten egg whites into chocolate mixture. Fold chocolate mixture into whipping cream. Chill and serve.

Serves 8

Lemon Mousse

Also try this light, tangy mousse as a lime variation, just substitute lime peel and juice. Adjust sugar to taste.

1 tbsp.	unflavoured gelatine (1 env.)	15 mL
2 tbsp.	cold water	30 mL
¼ cup	boiling water	60 mL
3	egg whites, beaten	3
½ cup	milk powder	125 mL
½ cup	water	125 mL
⅓ cup	sugar	75 mL
3 tbsp.	lemon juice	45 mL
1 tsp.	grated lemon peel	5 mL

1. Soften gelatine in cold water, about 10 minutes. Add boiling water to dissolve gelatine.
2. Mix egg whites with milk powder and water. Beat until stiff peaks form. Add gelatine and continue beating.
3. Combine sugar, lemon juice and half of the grated lemon peel. Mix well.
4. Fold into the egg white mixture.
5. Spoon mousse into individual glasses. Decorate with grated lemon peel.
6. Refrigerate, covered, until firm.

Serves 4

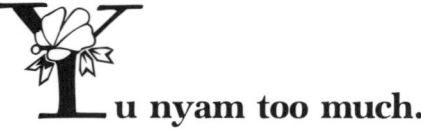

Yu nyam too much.

You eat too much.

White Wine Lemon Mousse with Raspberry Sauce

This raspberry sauce also adds vibrant colour and flavour to other fruit desserts and ice creams.

1 tbsp.	unflavoured gelatine (1 env.)	15 mL
2 tbsp.	white wine	30 mL
⅓ cup	lemon juice	75 mL
1½ tbsp.	grated lemon peel	22 mL
3	eggs, separated	3
8 tbsp.	sugar, divided	120 mL
1 cup	whipping cream, whipped	250 mL

RASPBERRY SAUCE:

10 oz.	pkg. frozen raspberries, thawed, drained	283 g
1 tbsp.	lemon juice	15 mL
2 tbsp.	sugar	30 mL
1 tbsp.	raspberry OR orange liqueur OR apricot brandy	15 mL
	mint sprigs for garnish	

1. In a small bowl, sprinkle gelatine over wine and let soften, about 10 minutes. Add lemon juice and peel, stir over simmering water until gelatine is dissolved.
2. In a medium bowl, beat egg yolks with 3 tbsp. (45 mL) sugar until yolks are light and lemon coloured. Stir in the gelatine mixture.
3. In a large bowl, beat egg whites until foamy; beat in 5 tbsp. (75 mL) sugar and beat until meringue holds soft peaks. Add whipped cream to egg yolk mixture and fold in half of meringue. Add cream mixture to remaining meringue and fold together. Chill mousse 3-4 hours.
4. To make the sauce, in a processor or blender, combine drained raspberries, lemon juice, sugar and liqueur; purée. Strain purée to remove seeds, if you prefer. Thin slightly with reserved raspberry juice.
5. Spoon the mousse into dessert dishes or wine glasses and drizzle sauce over each serving. Garnish with mint sprigs.

Serves 6

See photograph on page 51.

Soursop Mousse

A refreshing, tart and light dessert.

1	small soursop	1
1 cup	boiling water	250 mL
½ cup	sugar	125 mL
1 tbsp.	unflavoured gelatine (1 env.)	15 mL
2 tbsp.	water	30 mL
1 cup	evaporated milk	250 mL
1 tbsp.	lemon juice	15 mL
	mint sprigs for garnish	

1. Wash and peel soursop. Pour boiling water over the soursop pulp.
2. Soften the pulp with a food masher. Press the juice through a sieve.
3. Measure juice to 1 cup (250 mL); mix in sugar and cool.
4. Dissolve the gelatine in water. Add to the soursop juice.
5. Put milk in ice cube trays or a shallow pan and chill until crystals form around the edges.
6. Place milk in a bowl and whip until stiff. Add lemon juice to thickened milk. Stir in chilled soursop juice.
7. Put mousse mixture into a wet bowl. Chill until firm, about 3-4 hours.
8. Spoon mousse into dessert dishes or wine glasses and garnish each serving with mint sprigs.

Serves 4

See photograph on page 51.

Pineapple Fluff

Very quick and light; made with on-hand ingredients.

1 cup	evaporated milk	250 mL
14 oz.	can crushed pineapple	398 mL
1 tbsp.	unflavoured gelatine (1 env.)	15 mL
¼ cup	sugar	60 mL
	graham OR vanilla cookie crumbs	

Pineapple Fluff

(Continued)

1. Freeze evaporated milk.
2. Drain pineapple and reserve juice.
3. Bring 1 cup (250 mL) of pineapple juice and sugar to a boil.
4. Add softened gelatine; stir until gelatine is dissolved. Cool until slightly set.
5. Beat frozen milk until thick. Add gelatine mixture and whip to a fluff.
6. Fold in crushed pineapple. Pour into a dish and sprinkle with graham crumbs.
7. Chill until ready to serve.

Serves 4-6

Orange Fluff

Light and foamy texture, with real orange flavour.

2 tbsp.	unflavoured gelatine (2 env.)	30 mL
¼ cup	cold water	60 mL
½ cup	boiling water	125 mL
¾ cup	sugar	175 mL
1 cup	orange juice	250 mL
1 cup	evaporated milk, frozen	250 mL
2	oranges, pulp of	2

1. Soak gelatine in cold water to soften, about 10 minutes; add boiling water to dissolve.
2. Mix in sugar and orange juice. Refrigerate to set.
3. Beat in frozen milk until light and foamy.
4. Fold in orange pulp. Pour into a serving dish.
5. Chill until ready to serve.

Caramel Custard

A Crème Caramel with a hint of almond.

1¼ cups	sugar	300 mL
4	eggs	4
2½ cups	milk	625 mL
1 tsp.	almond extract	5 mL
¼ tsp.	salt	1 mL

1. In a skillet, heat ½ cup (125 mL) sugar over low heat until melted and golden brown. Watch carefully.
2. Pour caramelized sugar into a greased shallow casserole and swirl to coat the bottom of the dish.
3. In a bowl, beat eggs and ¾ cup (175 mL) sugar. Add milk, almond extract and salt, beating well.
4. Pour the egg mixture over the caramelized sugar.
5. Set the casserole into a shallow pan; pour hot water into the pan to come halfway up the sides of the casserole. Bake at 350°F (180°C) for 1½ hours, until a knife inserted in the centre of the custard comes out clean.
6. Remove the baked custard from the oven and from the pan of hot water. Cool for at least 3 hours.
7. To unmould, loosen the edges with a knife; invert custard onto a plate. The caramel will pool around the custard.

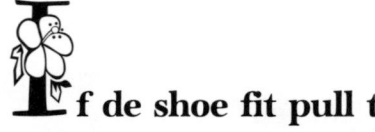

If de shoe fit pull the string.

If comments are made about you, only then respond.

Ginger Crème Brûlée

Ginger adds a zesty note to the rich creamy flavour of the classic Crème Brûlée

GINGER CUSTARD:

2 cups	whipping cream	500 mL
½ cup	sugar	125 mL
2 tbsp.	finely minced peeled fresh ginger	30 mL
1 tsp.	vanilla	5 mL
5	egg yolks	5
12 tsp.	white sugar OR packed brown sugar	60 mL
	sliced mango, papaya, kiwi, strawberries and/or pineapple	

1. Mix cream, sugar and ginger in a heavy medium saucepan. Stir over medium heat until sugar dissolves and mixture comes to a simmer. Cover pan; reduce heat to very low and simmer gently for 10 minutes to blend flavors. Add vanilla.
2. Preheat oven to 325°F (160°C). In a medium bowl, whisk yolks until well blended. Gradually whisk in hot cream mixture, just to blend. Divide custard mixture among 6, ¾ cup (175 mL) custard dishes. Place dishes in a shallow pan. Pour enough hot water into the pan to come halfway up sides of dishes. Carefully transfer pan to oven.
3. Bake until custards are almost set in the centre, gently shake the pan to test, about 35 minutes. Remove custards from the pan and cool for 30 minutes. Chill for 3-4 hours, up to 2 days.
4. To make the **Créme Brûlée**, sprinkle 2 tsp. (10 mL) of sugar evenly over each custard. Use a small kitchen blowtorch (the secret of professional chefs) to caramelize the sugar topping. Hold the blowtorch so that the flame is 2" (5 cm) above the sugar. Direct the flame to melt and brown the sugar, about 2 minutes **OR to broil**, preheat the broiler and broil until the sugar forms a crust. Watch carefully.
5. Refrigerate custards until they are firm but topping remains brittle, 2-4 hours. Garnish with your choice of fruit.

Serves 6

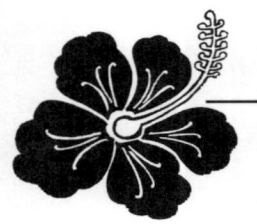

Brown Sugar Brûlée Crust

This make-ahead crust can also be used to top fruit and sour cream mixtures, ice cream, or use on Papaw Delight, page 26, or Caramelized Mango Cream, page 27.

butter
brown sugar

1. Cut aluminum foil circles the exact size of the dishes in which you are baking the brûlée. Butter 1 side of the foil and pat brown sugar to about ¼" (1 cm) thickness.
2. Place the foil circles on a cookie sheet under a preheated broiler until sugar is caramelized or glazed (slightly burnt). WATCH VERY CARE-FULLY.
3. Remove foil circles from the pan and cool, sugar side down, on cookie racks. Peel off foil when sugar is slightly cooled.
4. Place sugar disks (pralines) on Crème Brûlée just before serving.

Kheer – Rice Pudding

This East Indian rice pudding is very creamy and delicious.

1 cup	rice	250 mL
3 cups	water	750 mL
13½ oz.	can evaporated milk	385 mL
½, 10 oz.	can condensed milk	150 mL
	raisins and cherries	
¼ tsp.	cinnamon	1 mL
¼ tsp.	nutmeg	1 mL

1. In a small heavy saucepan, bring rice to a boil with 3 cups (750 mL) of water over low heat for about 20 minutes.
2. Add milk, raisins, cherries, cinnamon and nutmeg.
3. Transfer the pudding to an 8 x 12" (20 x 30 cm) ovenproof dish and bake at 250-300°F (120-150°C) for about 30 minutes.
4. Can be served warm or cold.

Serves 10

Trifle

Brought to the islands by the English, this traditional dessert is always popular. Tropical fruit adds an island touch.

1	sponge OR angel food cake	1
½ cup	sherry	125 mL
2 tbsp.	rum	30 mL
3 cups	evaporated milk	750 mL
½ cup	condensed milk	125 mL
1	lime, grated peel of	1
6	egg yolks	6
1½ tsp.	unflavoured gelatine (½ env.)	7 mL
1 tbsp.	vanilla	15 mL
1 tbsp.	custard powder	15 mL
2 tbsp.	milk	30 mL
2 cups	cubed papaya, mango, kiwi, strawberries, etc.	500 mL
1 cup	cubed pineapple	250 mL
2 cups	whipping cream, whipped sliced fruit for garnish	500 mL

1. Cube the sponge cake and place in a large bowl. Sprinkle sherry and rum over the sponge cubes.
2. Mix evaporated milk, condensed milk and lime peel. Bring to a boil over low heat.
3. Remove the milk mixture from the heat; slowly add slightly beaten egg yolks, gelatine and vanilla. Cook over low heat for 10 minutes.
4. Dissolve the custard powder in 2 tbsp. (30 mL) of milk. Add to egg mixture. Return to low heat. Cook until the custard is firm to touch.
5. Arrange half of soaked sponge pieces in a large glass bowl. Spoon over half of the custard mixture.
6. Spread half of the cubed fruit and the pineapple over the custard.
7. Repeat layers, beginning with sponge cake and followed by custard and fruit. Cover and chill for at least 3 hours.
8. Decorate with whipped cream and sliced fruit just before serving.

Serves 10

Chocolate & Banana Trifle

Chocolate custard, chocolate cake and chocolate shavings – how decadent, how delicious!

CHOCOLATE CUSTARD:

2 cups	whole milk	500 mL
½ cup	sugar	125 mL
5 oz.	semisweet chocolate, grated	140 g
2 tbsp.	cornstarch	30 mL
2 tbsp.	unsweetened cocoa	30 mL
4 tbsp.	water	60 mL
2	eggs	2
4	egg yolks	4
2 tbsp.	vanilla	30 mL
9 x 13"	chocolate cake	23 x 33 cm
4	ripe bananas, sliced	4
1 cup	whipping cream, whipped	250 mL
¼ cup	slivered, toasted almonds	60 mL
	raspberries OR sliced	
	strawberries for garnish	
	chocolate shavings for garnish	

1. To prepare the chocolate custard, place the milk, sugar and chocolate in a medium saucepan. Cook, stirring, over medium heat until the chocolate is melted and just about to boil.
2. Combine the cornstarch and cocoa. Add water and mix thoroughly. Stir the cornstarch mixture into the chocolate mixture. Whisk in the whole eggs and the extra egg yolks. Cook until thickened, about 5 minutes. Add the vanilla. Pour the custard into a bowl. Cover and chill.
3. Cube the chocolate cake. Layer half the cake in a large glass bowl. Arrange half of the banana slices around the sides of the bowl and on top of the cake. Spread half of the chocolate custard over the cake. Repeat cake, banana and the chocolate custard layers.
4. Whip the cream and spoon over the top layer of chocolate custard.
5. Chill trifle. Just before serving, sprinkle with slivered almonds and garnish with raspberries or sliced strawberries. Sprinkle with chocolate shavings.

Serves 10

Pies
&
Cheesecakes

No-Bake Strawberry Cream Pie

This "instant" dessert looks very pretty with the fresh strawberries.

GRAHAM CRUST:

3 tbsp.	butter	45 mL
1¼ cups	graham crumbs	300 mL
1 tbsp.	sugar	15 mL
1½ cups	cold milk	375 mL
3½ oz.	pkg. instant vanilla pudding	100 g
2 oz.	pkg. whipped topping mix	55 g
½ cup	strawberry jam	125 mL
	fresh strawberries, sliced	

1. Melt butter in a 9" (23 cm) pie plate over low heat. Stir in crumbs and sugar until blended. Press crumbs over bottom and sides of pie plate. Chill.
2. Combine milk, vanilla pudding and topping. Mix at low speed, then beat at high speed until peaks form.
3. Melt the strawberry jam; drizzle half of the jam over the bottom crust. Spoon in the pudding. Top with the remaining jam. Arrange sliced strawberries over the jam. Chill for about 3 hours before serving.

Serves 6-8

Yu cut yu nose to spite yu face.

If you do something to hurt someone, it will backfire.

Cream Cheese Fruit Pie

The glazed fruit sparkles on this dazzling pie.

**pastry for 9" (23 cm) pie shell,
see page 65, OR use a commercial
unbaked shell**

CITRUS CREAM CHEESE FILLING:

8 oz.	cream cheese, room temperature	250 g
¼ cup	sugar	60 mL
¼ cup	whipping cream	60 mL
1 tbsp.	fresh lemon OR lime juice	15 mL
1 tsp.	vanilla	5 mL
½	small pineapple, thinly sliced	½
3	kiwis, peeled, thinly sliced	3
1	large very ripe mango, peeled, thinly sliced	1
2 tbsp.	apricot OR peach preserves	30 mL

1. Place pastry in a 9" (23 cm) pie plate or in a flan or tart pan with a removable bottom. If using a flan pan, fold extra pastry in, forming double-thick sides, press firmly. Pierce the bottom of the crust with a fork. Bake at 425°F (220°C) until golden, about 14 minutes. Cool completely.
2. To make filling, beat cream cheese and sugar in a large bowl until smooth. Beat in whipping cream, juice and vanilla. Spread filling in prepared crust. Refrigerate until filling is firm, about 1 hour.
3. Arrange pineapple, kiwis and mango over filling. Melt preserves in a small saucepan over low heat. Brush preserves over fruit. Chill pie up to 2 hours.

Serves 8

Variations: *In season, use peaches, blueberries, strawberries and raspberries in addition to or to replace the fruit in this recipe.*

Brandied Ginger Fruit Tart

This rich cookie-like pastry is delicious with fruit tarts.

PÂTE SUCRÉE:

1¾ cups	all-purpose flour	425 mL
¼ cup	sugar	60 mL
¼ tsp.	salt	1 mL
10 tbsp.	chilled butter	150 mL
1	egg yolk	1
3 tbsp.	whipping cream	45 mL
½ tsp.	vanilla	2 mL

GINGER FILLING:

1 cup	whole milk	250 mL
3	egg yolks	3
⅓ cup	sugar	75 mL
2 tbsp.	cornstarch	30 mL
2 tbsp.	finely minced crystallized OR candied ginger	30 mL
⅔ cup	ginger preserves OR ginger marmalade	150 mL
2 tbsp.	brandy OR apricot brandy	30 mL
3	kiwis, thinly sliced	3
1	ripe papaya, thinly sliced	1
1	very ripe mango, thinly sliced mint sprigs for garnish	1

1. To make the crust, combine flour, sugar and salt in a processor. Cut in butter, using on/off turns, until mixture resembles coarse meal. In a small bowl, combine egg, cream and vanilla. Add to flour mixture; process just until dough comes together. Form dough into a flat disk, cover with plastic wrap and refrigerate for 4 hours or overnight.

Brandied Ginger Fruit Tart

(Continued)

2. To make the filling, pour milk into a heavy saucepan and bring to a simmer. Whisk yolks, sugar and cornstarch in a medium bowl; whisk in some of the hot milk and return to the saucepan. Whisk over medium heat until thickened. Pour the cooked filling into a bowl. Stir in the ginger and cover with plastic wrap. Refrigerate for 4 hours or overnight.
3. When ready to use, press dough over the bottom and up the sides of an 11" (28 cm) round flan or tart pan with a removable bottom. Line the crust with foil or waxed paper. Fill with dried beans or rice. Bake at 375°F (190°C) until the sides of the crust are set, about 15 minutes. Remove beans or rice and bake crust until golden and the bottom is set, about 15 minutes. Pierce the crust with a fork if it bubbles. Cool the crust on a rack; remove sides of pan.
4. Combine ginger preserves and brandy in a small saucepan. Melt preserves over medium heat. Strain ginger syrup into a small pan; discard solids. Brush half of ginger syrup over crust. Let stand at room temperature for about 5 minutes. Spread filling over crust. Arrange fruit over filling. Rewarm ginger syrup and brush over the fruit. Cover and chill for up to 2 hours. Garnish with mint sprigs just before serving.

Serves 8

See photograph on page 69.

Na mek mountain outa molehill.

Don't attach too much importance to little things.

Mango Pie

So easy and so good, this pie makes its own crust.

1	egg	1
½ tsp.	vanilla	2 mL
¾ cup	sugar	175 mL
½ cup	flour	125 mL
1 tsp.	baking powder	5 mL
¼ tsp.	salt	1 mL
1 cup	sliced, half-ripened mango	250 mL
½ cup	chopped walnuts	125 mL
¼ cup	flaked coconut	60 mL

1. In a small bowl, beat egg and add vanilla. Stir in ½ cup (125 mL) of sugar.
2. Combine flour, baking powder and salt; beat in egg mixture.
3. Add mango slices and walnuts, mixing well.
4. Pour egg/mango mixture into a well-greased 9" (23 cm) pie plate.
5. Sprinkle the remaining sugar and the coconut flakes over the mango filling.
6. Bake at 350°F (180°C) for 30-40 minutes.
7. Serve with whipped cream or ice cream.

Mango Tart Filling

Use this exotic mango filling for small tarts.

1	very large, very ripe mango or 2 small mangoes (about 1 lb. [500 g]), cut into ½" (1.3 cm) chunks	1
½ cup	sugar	125 mL
3 tbsp.	fresh lemon OR lime juice	45 mL
pinch	salt	pinch
4	egg yolks	4
¼ cup	butter, cut into small pieces	60 mL

Mango Tart Filling

(Continued)

1. In a food processor, purée mango, sugar, juice and salt. Add yolks and blend for 15 seconds. Strain over a large metal bowl; press on solids to extract as much purée as possible. Discard solids.
2. Set the metal bowl over a pan of simmering water, don't allow bowl to touch the water. Whisk the purée until thickened, about 10 minutes.
3. Remove from heat and whisk in butter, 1 piece at a time.
4. Cover and refrigerate overnight.

Yields about 1 cup (250 mL)

Guava Pie

Guavas are sweet and fragrant so this pie has a lovely flavour and aroma.

pastry for a 2-crust 9" (23 cm)
pie shell, see page 66

GUAVA FILLING:

4	guavas	4
6 tbsp.	flour	90 mL
³/₄ cup	sugar	175 mL
¹/₂ tsp.	salt	2 mL
¹/₂ tsp.	cinnamon	2 mL
2 tbsp.	butter OR margarine	30 mL
1 tbsp.	lemon juice	15 mL

1. Roll out half of the pastry and line a pie plate.
2. Wash, and cut guavas across. Scoop out guava halves with pulp intact, in cup shapes. Arrange guava cups on the pastry.
3. Mix together flour, sugar, salt, cinnamon, butter and lemon juice.
4. Pour mixture over fruit.
5. Roll out remaining pastry and cover the pie. Seal and flute the edges. Cut in steam vents.
6. Bake at 375°F (190°C) until fruit is cooked and pastry golden, about 30 minutes.

Coconut Pie

This creamy pie makes its own crust.

4	eggs	4
¼ lb.	butter, melted (½ cup [125 mL])	125 g
1 cup	sugar	250 mL
½ cup	self-rising flour	125 mL
1½ cups	milk	375 mL
1½ cups	shredded coconut	375 mL
2 tsp.	vanilla	10 mL

1. Beat eggs thoroughly. Add melted butter, sugar, flour and milk. Beat well with an electric mixer. Stir in coconut.
2. Pour into a 9½" (24 cm), lightly greased, pie plate. Bake at 350°F (180°C), for 35-40 minutes, until the top is golden and the centre is moist when pierced.
3. Let pie cool before slicing.

Serves 6

a put all yu hegg in one basket.

Diversify your investments.

Lime Daiquiri Pie

A daiquiri pie has the marvellous flavour of a daiquiri drink.

SINGLE CRUST PIE SHELL:

½ cup	butter	125 mL
¼ cup	cream cheese	60 mL
1¼ cups	flour	300 mL

LIME DAIQUIRI FILLING:

1 tbsp.	unflavoured gelatine (1 env.)	15 mL
⅔ cup	sugar	150 mL
¼ tsp.	salt	1 mL
¼ cup	fresh lime juice	60 mL
¼ cup	water	60 mL
3	egg yolks, slightly beaten	3
½ tsp.	finely shredded lime peel	2 mL
6	drops green food colouring	6
¼ cup	light rum	60 mL
3	egg whites	3
⅓ cup	sugar	75 mL
½ cup	whipping cream, whipped	125 mL
	lime slices for garnish	

1. To make the pastry, cut butter and cheese into flour until mixture resembles coarse crumbs. Form into a ball, wrap in plastic wrap and refrigerate for 1-2 hours.
2. Roll pastry on a lightly floured surface to form an 11" (28 cm) circle. Fit into a 9" (23 cm) pie plate, trim and flute edges. Prick the bottom and sides well with a fork.
3. Bake at 450°F (230°C) for 8-10 minutes. Cool.
4. In a small bowl, combine gelatine, sugar, salt, lime juice and water. Stir in beaten egg yolks; mix well. Cook and stir over low heat until gelatine dissolves and the mixture thickens.
5. Remove from the heat; add lime peel and food colouring. Cool. Stir in rum. Chill until partially set.
6. Beat egg whites to soft peaks, add sugar and beat to stiff peaks. Fold egg whites into the gelatine mixture and chill again.
7. Pile filling into the cooled pie shell. Chill until firm.
8. To serve, top pie with whipped cream and garnish with lime slices.

Raisin Cheddar Pie

Cheddar is a great flavour contrast with the rich sweetness of the raisins.

RAISIN FILLING:

½ cup	sugar	125 mL
4 tbsp.	cornstarch	60 mL
2 cups	raisins	500 mL
1½ cups	water	375 mL
¼ tsp.	salt	1 mL
1 tbsp.	butter OR margarine	15 mL
1	orange, grated peel, ½ juice of	1
1 tbsp.	lemon juice	15 mL
1 cup	grated Cheddar cheese	250 mL

TWO-CRUST PIE PASTRY:

2 cups	flour	500 mL
1 tsp.	salt	5 mL
⅔ cup	butter OR margarine	150 mL
6 tbsp.	cold water	90 mL
	milk	

1. To make the filling, combine sugar and cornstarch and blend well. Add raisins and water; cook over medium heat until thick.
2. Remove from the heat; add salt, butter, orange peel, orange juice and lemon juice. Mix well. Cool.
3. To make the pastry, stir together the flour and salt, cut in butter until the mixture resembles coarse meal.
4. Add cold water, a little at a time, until the mixture is moistened. Form dough into 2 balls.
5. Roll out 1 ball to 12" (30 cm) diameter. Transfer to 9" (23 cm) pie plate.
6. Pour the filling into the uncooked pastry shell. Sprinkle the cheese over the filling.
7. Roll out the second ball of dough for the top crust.
8. Cover the pie with the pastry; trim off excess dough. Flute edges and cut steam vents in pastry. Brush crust with a little milk.
9. Bake at 375°F (190°C) for 15-20 minutes.

Lime Cheesecake with Crystallized Ginger Crust

Crystallized ginger adds real snap to this tropical cheesecake.

CRYSTALLIZED GINGER CRUST:

1⅓ cups	gingersnap cookie crumbs	325 mL
½ cup	finely chopped toasted macadamia nuts	125 mL
¼ cup	packed golden brown sugar	60 mL
2 tbsp.	minced crystallized ginger	30 mL
2 tbsp.	melted butter	30 mL

LIME FILLING:

4 x 8 oz.	cream cheese, softened	4 x 250 g
1½ cups	sugar	375 mL
1 tbsp.	finely minced lime peel	15 mL
⅔ cup	sour cream	150 mL
6 tbsp.	fresh lime juice	90 mL
4	eggs	4
1	mango, sliced	1
3	kiwis, sliced	3
4	large strawberries, sliced	4
1	small pineapple, thinly sliced mint sprigs for garnish	1

1. To make the crust, butter a 9" (23 cm) springform pan. With a fork, blend all crust ingredients until moistened. Press crumb mixture over the bottom and partway up sides of pan. Bake at 350°F (1870°C) about 8 minutes. Cool on a rack.
2. To make the filling, using an electric mixer, beat cream cheese, sugar and lime peel in large bowl until light and fluffy. Beat in sour cream and lime juice. Add eggs, 1 at a time, beating just until blended.
3. Pour the filling into the crust. Bake until cheesecake edges are firm but centre moves slightly when pan is shaken, about 1 hour and 20 minutes. Cool on a rack for 10 minutes. Cover and chill overnight.
4. To serve, remove pan sides and arrange mango, kiwi, strawberries and pineapple on top of the cheesecake. Garnish with mint sprigs.

Serves 12

No-Bake Tropical Cheesecake

This very simple, no-bake cheesecake can be garnished with any fresh fruit.

1¼ cups	graham crumbs	300 mL
¼ cup	butter	60 mL
¼ cup	icing sugar	60 mL
2 cups	whipping cream	500 mL
1 cup	cream cheese (8 oz. [250 g])	250 mL
1 cup	icing (confectioner's) sugar	250 mL
2-3 cups	chopped or sliced mango, kiwi, pineapple or papaya	500-750 mL

1. Combine graham crumbs with melted butter and icing sugar. Spread evenly over the bottom of a 9" (23 cm) springform pan or square baking dish pan. Refrigerate for 1-3 hours.
2. Whip cream until firm.
3. Slowly beat in cream cheese and icing sugar.
4. Spread filling over graham crumbs. Refrigerate for 1 hour.
5. Arrange drained fruit on cheesecake. Chill for several hours. Cut into wedges or squares to serve.

Serves 10

ye na see haat na bun.

If I have no knowledge of this I will not be upset.

Brandied Ginger Fruit Tart, page 60

Sweets

Jalebi

These East Indian treats are very sweet. They absorb the lovely flavour of the rose syrup.

1 tsp.	sugar	5 mL
1 tbsp.	warm water	15 mL
1 tbsp.	yeast	15 mL
2 cups	flour	500 mL
2 tsp.	rice flour	10 mL
1 cup	water OR a bit more or less for proper consistency	250 mL
	oil for frying	

1. Dissolve sugar in warm water. Add yeast and leave for 10 minutes.
2. Stir in flour and rice flour with enough water to make a medium batter. Set aside for 1 hour.
3. Place oil to a depth of 1" (2.5 cm) in a frying pan. Heat oil to 400°F (200°C). Pipe batter mixture through a funnel (¼" [1 cm] in diameter) forming small concentric circles. Fry until golden brown, about ½ minute on each side. Place Jalebi on paper towels to drain.

ROSE SYRUP:

2½ cups	sugar	625 mL
1½ cups	water	375 mL
¼ tsp.	yellow or red food colouring	1 mL
½ tsp.	rose essence	2 mL

1. In a small saucepan, combine sugar, water, food colouring and rose essence. Boil until thick.
2. Place Jalebi in warm syrup. When thoroughly soaked with syrup, remove and set aside.

See photograph on page 51.

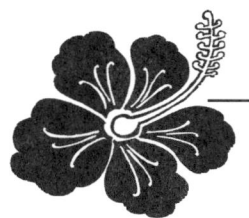

Gulab Jamoon

These golden sweet balls are truly delicious with the added flavour of the spicy/sweet cardamom syrup.

1 cup	skim milk powder	250 mL
¼ cup	flour	60 mL
1 tsp.	baking powder	5 mL
1 tbsp.	butter OR margarine	15 mL
1	egg yolk	1
¼ cup	milk, more or less as needed for dough consistency	60 mL
	oil for frying	

1. Combine milk powder, flour, baking powder and butter until the mixture resembles bread crumbs.
2. Stir in egg yolk and just enough milk to make a soft dough. Knead well, until dough is not sticky.
3. Set dough aside for 1 hour. Rub vegetable oil on the palms of your hands. Shape the dough into 30 small round balls.
4. In a deep pan, heat oil to 375°F (190°C). Deep-fry over medium heat, a few at a time, until evenly browned.
5. Place cooked balls on paper towels to drain.

CARDAMOM SYRUP:

2 cups	white sugar	500 mL
2 cups	water	500 mL
½ tsp.	vanilla	2 mL
2	cardamom pods	2
2 drops	yellow food colouring	2 drops

1. In a large heavy saucepan, combine all syrup ingredients; bring to a boil and cook until mixture is slightly sticky.
2. Place the balls in the syrup. Boil for 5 minutes; cover and let stand for about 6 hours.

Variation: *Garnish with edible silver foil and/or slivered pistachios for an elegant presentation, see page 103.*

See photograph on page 103.

Ghul-Ghula

These spongy spiced balls are the Guyana and Trinidad versions of small doughnut balls.

1 cup	flour	250 mL
1½ tsp.	baking powder	7 mL
⅛ tsp.	salt	0.5 mL
1 tbsp.	butter OR margarine	15 mL
½ cup	sugar	125 mL
½ tsp.	nutmeg	2 mL
¼ cup	raisins	60 mL
1	egg, beaten	1
½ tsp.	vanilla	2 mL
⅓ cup	milk	75 mL
	oil for frying	

1. Sift flour; add baking powder and salt.
2. Cut in butter until mixture resembles coarse crumbs.
3. Stir in sugar, nutmeg and raisins.
4. Add beaten egg, vanilla and just enough milk to mix to a soft smooth consistency.
5. Place oil to a depth of 1" (2.5 cm) in a deep pan or frying pan and heat oil to 375°F (190°C). Carefully drop batter, 1 tbsp. (15 mL) at a time, into hot oil; fry until golden.
6. Place cooked Ghul-Ghula on paper towels to drain off excess oil.

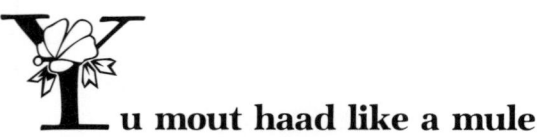

Yu mout haad like a mule.

You are a very stubborn person.

Rasmalai

These East Indian cheese curd balls are poached in sugar syrup and drizzled with a Cardamom-Saffron Sauce.

PANEER (CREAM CHEESE):

8 cups	milk	2 L
2 tsp.	vinegar	10 mL
4 tsp.	flour	20 mL

SUGAR SYRUP:

2 cups	sugar	500 mL
4 cups	water	1 L

CARDAMOM-SAFFRON SAUCE:

4 cups	milk	1 L
1 tbsp.	sugar	15 mL
¼ tsp.	freshly crushed cardamom	1 mL
pinch	saffron	pinch

1. **To make the paneer**, in a saucepan, bring the milk to a boil. Remove milk from heat and add a little vinegar. Stir gently until the milk curdles.
2. Place muslin over a colander and pour in the curdled milk; draw the muslin into a bag; squeeze gently to remove water.
3. On a board; knead the paneer (cheese) until it becomes smooth and soft.
4. Add the flour and knead thoroughly again. Shape the paneer (cheese) into round balls or flat oval pieces.
5. **To make the syrup**, in a large saucepan, dissolve the sugar in the water. Bring to a boil. Gently slip in the paneer balls. Boil for 15-20 minutes over medium heat.
6. When the cheese balls float, remove them from the syrup and drain.
7. **To make the sauce**, in a small saucepan, combine the milk, sugar and cardamom; boil for 5 minutes over low heat, until thickened. Let the sauce cool.
8. To serve, arrange the paneer balls in a dish and pour the cooled syrup over them.

Peera

Peera is like a creamy white fudge.

13½ oz.	evaporated milk	385 mL
1 cup	sugar	250 mL
1 tbsp.	butter	15 mL
1½ cups	whole milk powder	375 mL

1. In a saucepan, heat the milk and add the sugar, stirring to dissolve. Bring to a boil, adding butter. Boil over medium heat for about 5 minutes.
2. Add the milk powder gradually; constantly stirring over low heat for about 1 hour, until the mixture becomes thick.
3. Remove the milk mixture from the heat and continue beating.
4. While still warm, roll ½ tbsp. (7 mL) of the dough, in the palm of your hand, into a round ball. Repeat until all Peera are shaped. Store in an air-tight container at room temperature.

very rope gat two ends.

Every story has two sides.

Coconut No-Bake Cakes from Guyana & Trinidad

These small sugar cakes are a bit like tiny rich coconut macaroons.

1 cup	sugar	250 mL
1 cup	water	250 mL
4 cups	grated coconut	1 L
½ tsp.	cream of tartar	2 mL
1 tsp.	almond OR vanilla extract	5 mL
2-3	drops of food colouring (optional)	2-3

1. In a small saucepan, boil sugar and water to form a light syrup. When small bubbles appear in the syrup, add grated coconut and cream of tartar.
2. When the coconut mixture pulls away from the sides of the pan easily, remove from the heat and beat with a wooden spoon for 3-5 minutes. Mix in almond flavouring and food colouring.
3. Drop the dough by small spoonfuls on an oiled cookie sheet. Allow to set completely.
4. Store the cakes in an airtight container at room temperature.

Variations: *Colour half of the dough with strawberry food colouring and leave the other half white. Place a thin layer of pink dough on top of the white to make two-tone sugar cakes.*

Every best friend get a next best friend.

Your secrets are spread from best friend to best friend.

Pineapple Bars

Easy to make, these are very satisfying with a delicate, crunchy coconut topping.

1 cup	flour	250 mL
1 tsp.	baking powder	5 mL
¼ cup	butter OR margarine	60 mL
2	eggs	2
1 tbsp.	milk	15 mL
19 oz.	can crushed pineapple, drained	540 mL
2 tbsp.	melted butter OR margarine	30 mL
1 cup	sugar	250 mL
1 cup	flaked coconut	250 mL
1 tsp.	vanilla	5 mL

1. Sift flour and baking powder together. Cut in butter until mixture is crumbly.
2. Beat 1 egg with milk; stir into flour mixture.
3. Spread crust mixture evenly in an 8" (20 cm) square baking pan.
4. Top with crushed pineapple.
5. Beat the remaining egg; stir in melted butter, sugar, flaked coconut and vanilla.
6. Spread the coconut topping over the pineapple.
7. Bake at 350°F (180°C) for 35-40 minutes.
8. Cool and cut into 16 squares.

Yields 16 squares

If yuh eye nah see, yuh mouth nah must talk.

You must see for yourself before you speak.

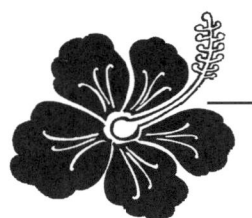

Milk Barfi

Barfi or Burfi is a traditional East Indian sweet-meat.

2¼ cups	milk	550 mL
1½ cups	sugar	375 mL
1 cup	milk powder	250 mL
1 cup	unsalted butter	250 mL
6-8	cardamom pods, crushed	6-8
	few drops of rose water	
	slivers of almonds OR pistachios for decoration	

1. Boil 2 cups (500 mL) of milk and 1½ cups (375 mL) of sugar until the mixture becomes thick.
2. Mix the remaining milk with milk powder and stir into the milk and sugar mixture.
3. Add butter, cardamom and rose water, beating until the mixture thickens.
4. Press the milk mixture into an 8" (20 cm) square greased pan. Decorate with almonds.
5. When cool cut into diamond shapes.

Variations: *Shreds of edible silver foil, available in East or West Indian grocery stores, make a very elegant decoration.*

**f yuh plant plantain yuh can't reap cassava.**

You reap what you sow.

Cake Vermicelli

Different and delicious, both the texture and the flavour of this cake are unique.

¼ cup	butter	60 mL
8 oz.	vermicelli (fine pasta), broken	250 g
4 cups	milk	1 L
½ cup	sugar	125 mL
½ tsp.	vanilla	2 mL
⅓ cup	raisins	75 mL
2 tbsp.	maraschino cherries	30 mL
½ tsp.	ground cardamom	2 mL
1 tsp.	grated nutmeg	5 mL

1. Heat the butter in a heavy skillet; add the vermicelli and stir gently until it becomes golden brown.
2. Pour in the milk and slowly bring to a boil. Boil over medium heat until the vermicelli is tender, about 5-7 minutes.
3. Add sugar to taste; add vanilla, raisins, cherries, ground cardamom and nutmeg.
4. Continue boiling the vermicelli mixture until it thickens and starts to set.
5. Pour the vermicelli mixture into a 7 x 10" (18 x 25 cm) baking dish. When cool cut into squares.

Serves 18

Variation: To bake, *after adding the cardamom and nutmeg, pour into a 7 x 10" (18 x 25 cm) glass baking dish and bake at 325°F (160°C) for about 45 minutes, until firm but still soft. Remove from the oven and cool. Cut into squares to serve.*

Cakes
&
Loaves

Pineapple Upside-Down Cake

As this cake bakes, the pineapple juice and sugar caramelize to form a delicious topping.

³/₄ cup	butter	175 mL
1 cup	sugar	250 mL
3	eggs	3
2 cups	flour	500 mL
2 tsp.	baking powder	10 mL
¹/₂ tsp.	salt	2 mL
¹/₂ cup	pineapple juice	125 mL
1 tsp.	vanilla	5 mL
¹/₂ cup	brown sugar	125 mL
14 oz.	can crushed pineapple, drained	398 mL
6-8	maraschino cherries, halved	6-8

1. Cream butter well, add sugar slowly and cream with the butter. Beat in eggs.
2. Sift flour, baking powder and salt; add to egg mixture. Beat until smooth.
3. Stir in pineapple juice and vanilla.
4. Prepare a greased 8 x 12" (20 x 30 cm) pan, covering the bottom with grease-proof paper. Sprinkle with brown sugar and cover with crushed pineapple, decorate with cherry halves.
5. Pour the cake batter over the fruit. Bake at 325°F (160°C) for 40-45 minutes.
6. Turn the cake over on a cake rack covered with waxed paper or foil, to catch the drips. Remove the grease-proof paper from the top of the cake. Cool and serve.

Carrot Cake

Always popular, this Caribbean Carrot Cake version includes pineapple and coconut.

2 cups	flour	500 mL
2 tsp.	baking powder	10 mL
1½ tsp.	baking soda	7 mL
1 tsp.	salt	5 mL
2 tsp.	cinnamon	10 mL
1½ cups	vegetable oil	375 mL
2 cups	sugar	500 mL
4	eggs	4
2 cups	grated carrots	500 mL
19 oz.	can drained, crushed pineapple	540 mL
½ cup	crushed walnuts	250 mL
½ cup	finely grated coconut	250 mL

1. In a large bowl, combine flour, baking powder, baking soda, salt, cinnamon and sugar. Beat with an electric mixer. Add oil and sugar, mixing well until fluffy.
2. Stir in carrots, pineapple, walnuts and coconut.
3. Pour the batter into a greased 9 x 13" (23 x 33 cm) pan and bake at 350°F (180°C) for about 45 minutes.
4. Cool cake and frost with Cream Cheese Icing, page 84.

Serves 12-16

Yuh can't suck cane and blow whistle.

Do not try to carry out two tasks at the same time.

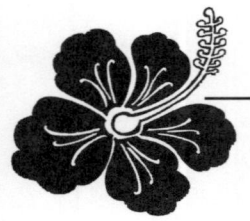

Cream Cheese Icing

This basic icing is creamy and delicious.

8 oz.	cream cheese	250 g
½ cup	butter OR margarine	125 mL
2 tsp.	vanilla	10 mL
1 cup	sifted icing (confectioner's) sugar	250 mL

1. Beat together the cream cheese, butter and vanilla; add enough sugar to give the icing a good spreading consistency.

Yields about 2 cups (500 mL)

Caribbean Citrus Icing

Orange-flavoured liqueur and lime juice add a tropical touch to a classic icing.

4 oz.	cream cheese	125 g
5 tsp.	milk	25 mL
1 lb.	icing (confectioner's) sugar	500 g
2 tbsp.	Curaçao OR Cointreau	30 mL
1	lime, grated peel of	1
1 tsp.	lime juice	5 mL

1. Beat together the cream cheese and milk.
2. Gradually beat in remaining ingredients until desired consistency is reached. Add more sugar or milk as needed.

Yields about 2 cups (500 mL)

Coconut Cake

Very moist and very easy.

3 cups	flour	750 mL
½ tsp.	salt	2 mL
4 tsp.	baking powder	20 mL
1 cup	butter OR margarine	250 mL
1½ cups	sugar	375 mL
1¼ cups	grated coconut	325 mL
4	eggs, well beaten	4
¾ cup	milk	175 mL

1. In a large bowl, sift flour, salt and baking powder; add butter and cut with 2 knives until mixture resembles fine bread crumbs.
2. Stir in sugar and coconut; mix well.
3. Slowly add beaten eggs; stir thoroughly.
4. Add milk and mix well.
5. Pour the batter into a greased 9 x 13" (23 x 33 cm) pan and bake at 325°F (160°C) for about 1½ hours, until golden brown and firm to the touch. Turn out and cool.
6. To serve, sprinkle with powdered sugar or frost with a butter or cream cheese frosting, see pages 84, 87 or 95.

Yuh can't drink mauby and belch beer.

If you put little effort in a task you can expect very little success.

Ginger Coconut Cake

The spicy flavours of this cake are a tropical treat.

2 cups + 3 tbsp.	sifted all-purpose flour	545 mL
2 tsp.	baking powder	10 mL
¾-1 tsp.	ground ginger	3-5 mL
¾ tsp.	baking soda	3 mL
¾ tsp.	salt	3 mL
1 tsp.	ground cinnamon	5 mL
1 cup	butter	250 mL
¾ cup	sugar	175 mL
2	eggs	2
10 tbsp.	light molasses	150 mL
2 tbsp.	grated orange peel	30 mL
1 tsp.	vanilla	5 mL
¾ cup	buttermilk	175 mL
1 cup	toasted shredded sweetened coconut	250 mL
½ cup	finely diced candied OR crystallized ginger	125 mL
	sliced pineapple, papaya, mango and/or kiwi for garnish	

1. Butter 2, 9" (23 cm) layer cake pans. Line with waxed paper; butter and flour the paper.
2. In a medium bowl, sift flour, baking powder, ginger, baking soda, salt and cinnamon.
3. Using an electric mixer, cream butter and sugar in a large bowl until fluffy. Beat in eggs 1 at a time. Add molasses, orange peel and vanilla; beat 1 minute on high until well-blended.
4. Mix in dry ingredients alternately with buttermilk, beginning and ending with dry ingredients. Fold in coconut and ginger.
5. Divide batter between prepared pans. Bake at 350°F (180°C) until firm to the touch, about 30 minutes. Cool in pans on a rack for 5 minutes. Invert cakes onto racks. Remove paper and cool completely.
6. Prepare the Ginger Cream Cheese Icing on page 87.
7. Place 1 cake layer on a cake plate, flat side down. Spread with ¼ of the icing. Top with the second cake layer. Spread remaining icing over top and sides of cake. When serving, garnish with sliced fruit.

Serves 12

Ginger Cream Cheese Icing

Ginger and orange are a superb combination.

8 oz.	cream cheese	250 g
½ cup	butter	125 mL
2 tbsp.	grated orange peel	30 mL
1 tsp.	vanilla	5 mL
1 lb.	icing (confectioner's) sugar	500 g
⅓ cup	finely minced candied OR crystallized ginger	75 mL

1. Using an electric mixer, beat cream cheese and butter until smooth. Mix in orange peel and vanilla. Beat in sugar. Mix in ginger.

Cassava Pone

This popular Caribbean dessert combines cassava and coconut. No flour is needed as the cassava supplies the starch.

2	medium, sweet cassava	2
1	small, dried coconut	1
2 tbsp.	butter	30 mL
½ cup	sugar	125 mL
½ tsp.	allspice	2 mL
½ tsp.	salt	2 mL
½ tsp.	vanilla	2 mL
2 cups	water	500 mL

1. Peel, wash and grate cassava. Grate coconut. Mix both with butter in a medium bowl.
2. Add sugar, allspice, salt and vanilla. Mix well. Add enough water to make a stiff batter.
3. Pour batter into a shallow, greased 8" (20 cm) square pan and bake at 250°F (120°C) for about 1½ hours. The top should be brown and crisp.
4. Cool. Cut in 2" (5 cm) squares before serving.

Spicy Gingerbread

Crystallized ginger adds extra flavour and texture to this spicy treat.

2 cups	flour	500 mL
2 tsp.	baking powder	10 mL
1 tsp.	baking soda	5 mL
½ tsp.	salt	2 mL
1 tsp.	allspice	5 mL
1 cup	unsalted butter	250 mL
½ cup	brown sugar	125 mL
1 cup	molasses	250 mL
1 cup	evaporated milk	250 mL
2	eggs, well-beaten	2
2 tsp.	ground ginger	10 mL
2 tbsp.	finely chopped crystallized ginger	30 mL

1. In a small bowl, sift dry ingredients together.
2. Melt the butter. In a large bowl, mix butter with sugar, molasses, milk and eggs.
3. Add dry ingredients, blending thoroughly.
4. Fold in ground ginger and crystallized ginger.
5. Pour batter into a greased 5 x 9" (13 x 23 cm) loaf pan and bake at 350°F (180°C) for 45 minutes.
6. Serve with Vanilla Custard Sauce, below.

VANILLA CUSTARD SAUCE:

1 cup	milk	250 mL
2	eggs	2
2 tbsp.	sugar	30 mL
½ tsp.	vanilla	2 mL

1. Heat milk in the top of a double boiler.
2. In a small bowl, beat eggs, add sugar. Blend well.
3. Stir some of the hot milk into the egg mixture. Pour the egg mixture into the hot milk in the top of the double boiler. When thickened, add vanilla. Cool.

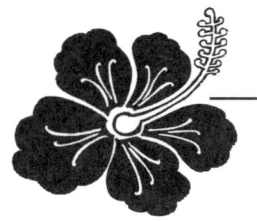

Ginger Pound Cake

A very dense, flavourful, traditional pound cake.

1 cup	butter	250 mL
1¹/₃ cups	fruit (berry) sugar	325 mL
4	eggs	4
1	lemon, juice of (2 tbsp. [30 mL])	1
1 tsp.	vanilla	5 mL
4 oz.	candied ginger in heavy syrup, drained, finely chopped	115 g
2 cups	cake (pastry) flour	500 mL

1. In a medium bowl, with an electric mixer, cream butter and sugar well. Beat in eggs 1 at a time.
2. Beat in lemon juice and vanilla.
3. Stir in candied ginger.
4. Stir in flour, just until thoroughly mixed.
5. Pour batter into a greased, waxed paper-lined 5 x 9" (12 x 23 cm) loaf pan and bake at 300°F (150°C) for 1³/₄-2 hours.

Yields 1 loaf

Variation: *For added ginger flavour, pierce the hot baked cake all over with a skewer and pour the drained ginger syrup over it before removing from the loaf pan.*

ne, one dutty build dam.

Every little bit adds up.

Lemon Pound Cake

This light pound cake has a fluffier texture because the egg whites are beaten separately and folded into the batter.

2 cups	butter OR margarine	500 mL
2 cups	sugar	500 mL
8	large eggs, separated	8
2 cups	flour	500 mL
1 tsp.	baking powder	5 mL
½ tsp.	salt	2 mL
½ tsp.	grated lemon peel	2 mL
2 tbsp.	lemon juice	30 mL
½ tsp.	lemon extract	2 mL

1. In a medium bowl, with an electric mixer, cream butter and sugar well; add beaten egg yolks.
2. Add flour, baking powder and salt, beating until smooth.
3. Beat the egg whites until stiff but not dry.
4. Fold the beaten egg whites, lemon peel, lemon juice and extract into the batter.
5. Pour batter into a greased 5 x 9" (12 x 23 cm) loaf pan and bake at 325°F (180°C) for about 1-1½ hours.

Hard times mek sheep an' goat graze ah one pasture.

Adversity can create strange bedfellows.

Mango Cake

Mango adds colour and tropical flavour to this loaf cake.

½ cup	butter OR margarine	125 mL
1 cup	sugar	250 mL
2	eggs	2
1 cup	mashed, ripe mango	250 mL
1½ cups	flour	375 mL
2 tsp.	baking powder	10 mL
½ tsp.	allspice	2 mL
1 tsp.	vanilla	5 mL
1 tbsp.	cream	15 mL
½ cup	chopped nuts, walnuts OR pecans	125 mL

1. In a medium bowl, cream butter and sugar; add eggs 1 at a time, beating well.
2. Add mango and mix in thoroughly.
3. Combine flour, baking powder and allspice, stir into mango mixture. Stir in vanilla, cream and nuts.
4. Pour batter into a greased 5 x 9" (13 x 23 cm) loaf pan and bake at 350°F (180°C) for 40-50 minutes.

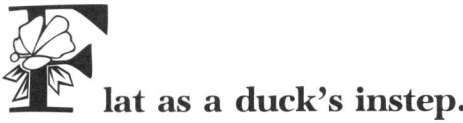

Flat as a duck's instep.

Being broke, having no money.

Banana Cake

Moist and very flavourful – always a favourite.

¾ cup	butter OR margarine	175 mL
1 cup	sugar	250 mL
3	eggs, beaten	3
2 tsp.	almond extract	10 mL
1 cup	mashed banana	250 mL
1¼ cups	flour	300 mL
1 tsp.	baking powder	5 mL
1 tsp.	baking soda	5 mL
¼ tsp.	ground cinnamon	1 mL

1. In a medium bowl, cream together butter and sugar.
2. Add beaten eggs and almond extract, mixing well.
3. Add mashed banana.
4. Sift remaining dry ingredients and fold into creamed mixture.
5. Pour batter into an 8" (20 cm) square pan and bake at 350°F (180°C) for 20-25 minutes.

Kyarri it yaso.

Bring it here.

Orange Sponge Cake

Orange juice and peel add flavour to the batter and the filling.

1¼ cups	flour	300 mL
1½ tsp.	baking powder	7 mL
½ tsp.	salt	2 mL
3	eggs, separated	3
1 cup	sugar	250 mL
½ cup	orange juice	125 mL
2 tsp.	grated orange peel	10 mL
¼ tsp.	cream of tartar	1 mL

1. In a small bowl, sift together the flour, baking powder and salt.
2. In a large bowl, beat egg yolks well, until thick and pale in colour. Gradually beat in sugar.
3. Add orange juice and peel; fold in the sifted ingredients.
4. In a separate bowl, beat egg whites and cream of tartar until stiff. Fold into the batter.
5. Pour batter into 2 layer pans and bake at 325°F (160°C) for about 20 minutes.
6. Cool cake layers before filling with the Orange Filling below.
7. If you want to ice this cake, use a Cream Cheese Icing, page 84, or the Lemon Butter Cream Icing on page 95.

ORANGE FILLING:

¼ cup	sugar	60 mL
1½ tbsp.	flour	22 mL
¼ tsp.	salt	1 mL
¼ cup	orange juice	60 mL
2 tsp.	grated orange peel	10 mL
1	egg yolk	1
2 tsp.	butter	10 mL
1 tsp.	lemon juice	5 mL

1. Place sugar, flour and salt in the top of a double boiler. Add orange juice and peel. Mix well.
2. Add egg yolk and butter; stir and cook until smooth and thick.
3. Remove the filling from the heat. Add lemon juice and cool. Spread between cake layers.

93

Lemon Torte

This torte has a crisp cookie crust layer, 2 sponge cake layers and a luscious lemon icing.

1 cup	butter	250 mL
2 cups	flour	500 mL
¹/₂ cup	sugar	125 mL
9	eggs, separated	9
1¹/₄ cups	sugar	300 mL
2 tbsp.	orange juice concentrate	60 mL
¹/₄ cup	melted butter	60 mL
1 cup	flour	250 mL
	Lemon Butter Cream Icing, page 95	
³/₄ cup	tart jam (raspberry, blackberry OR red currant, etc.)	175 mL
1 cup	cubed pineapple OR mango OR mandarin orange sections pineapple, mango OR orange slices for garnish	250 mL

1. Mix butter, sifted flour and sugar with a pastry blender until crumbly. Press into a greased 11" (28 cm) springform pan. Bake at 350°F (180°C) for 20 minutes.
2. When the crust is cool; remove from pan and place on a cake plate.
3. In a large bowl, beat egg yolks with ³/₄ cup (175 mL) of sugar until light and lemon coloured. Add orange juice and melted butter. Fold in flour.
4. In a separate bowl, beat egg whites with ¹/₂ cup (125 mL) sugar until stiff. Fold the egg whites into the egg yolk mixture.
5. Pour the batter into 2 greased 11" (28 cm) springform pans. Bake at 350°F (180°C) for about 20 minutes. Cool.
6. Prepare the Lemon Butter Cream Icing on the next page.

Lemon Torte

(Continued)

7. **To assemble the cake**, heat the jam to make a glaze. Spread the bottom crust layer with ½ cup (125 mL) of the jam.
8. Place one sponge layer on top of the jam layer; spread with a thin layer of Lemon Butter Cream; arrange pineapple pieces or mandarin oranges over the butter cream.
9. Place the second layer of sponge cake on top of the fruit. Cover the top and sides with butter cream. Decorate with fruit. Melt the remaining jam and brush over the fruit to glaze.

See photograph on page 103.

Lemon Butter Cream Icing

This rich icing has an intense lemon flavour.

4 oz.	lemon pie filling, cooked variety	113 g
1	egg	1
½ lb.	unsalted butter, softened	250 g
1½ cups	icing (confectioner's) sugar	375 mL

1. Prepare lemon pie filling according to package directions, adding the egg. Cover and cool to room temperature.
2. Cream butter with icing sugar. Add lemon filling. Beat until smooth and stiff. Add more icing sugar, if needed, for a firmer icing.

Cherry Chiffon Cake

This light cake is a lovely colour.

2 cups	flour	500 mL
1¼ cups	sugar	300 mL
3 tsp.	baking powder	15 mL
½ tsp.	salt	2 mL
½ cup	vegetable oil	125 mL
½ cup	water	125 mL
5	eggs, separated	5
2 tsp.	almond extract	10 mL
½ tsp.	cream of tartar	2 mL
1 cup	chopped maraschino cherries	250 mL

1. In a large bowl, mix flour, sugar, baking powder and salt.
2. Add vegetable oil, water, egg yolks and almond extract; beat until smooth.
3. In a separate bowl, beat egg whites and cream of tartar until very stiff.
4. Gradually fold the egg white mixture into the batter.
5. Gently stir in the cherries.
6. Pour the batter into an ungreased 10" (25 cm) tube pan; bake at 325°F (160°C) for 1 hour.
7. Invert the pan immediately and leave suspended until cold, carefully remove the cake from the pan.

u dun yet?

Have you finished?

Brown Sugar Chocolate Cake

In the islands and around the world, chocolate is an all-time favourite. This cake is easy and very good.

³/₄ cup	butter OR margarine	175 mL
³/₄ cup	brown sugar	175 mL
4	eggs	4
2 tsp.	vanilla	10 mL
1¹/₄ cups	flour	300 mL
4 tbsp.	cocoa	60 mL
2 tsp.	baking powder	10 mL
¹/₄ tsp.	salt	1 mL
³/₄ cup	milk	175 mL

1. In a large bowl, cream butter and sugar until fluffy, with an electric mixer.
2. Add eggs 1 at a time, beating well after each addition. Stir in vanilla.
3. Sift flour, cocoa, baking powder and salt.
4. Add to butter mixture, alternating with milk.
5. Pour batter into 9" (23 cm) greased layer pans and bake at 325°C (160 mL) for 30-35 minutes. Chocolate Butter Icing or raspberry or apricot jam may be used to put layers together.

Chocolate Butter Icing

Coffee and cinnamon add a taste of the tropics.

3 oz.	unsweetened chocolate	85 g
2 tbsp.	butter OR margarine	30 mL
¹/₄ cup	hot coffee OR milk OR water	60 mL
¹/₄ tsp.	cinnamon or to taste (optional)	1 mL
¹/₈ tsp.	salt	0.5 mL
2 cups	icing (confectioner's) sugar or more as needed	500 mL
1 tsp.	vanilla	5 mL

1. In a large bowl, melt chocolate and butter together.
2. Stir in hot coffee, cinnamon, if using, and salt.
3. Gradually beat in icing sugar to desired consistency. Beat in vanilla.

Rum & Raisin Cake

Brown Sugar Raisin Filling adds texture and great flavour.

RUM CAKE:

½ cup	butter OR margarine	125 mL
½ cup	sugar	125 mL
3	eggs	3
1⅓ cups	flour	325 mL
2 tsp.	baking powder	10 mL
¼ cup	rum	60 mL

BROWN SUGAR RAISIN FILLING:

2 tbsp.	butter OR margarine	30 mL
½ cup	brown sugar	125 mL
3 tbsp.	flour	45 mL
½ cup	raisins	125 mL

1. In a large bowl, with an electric mixer, cream butter with sugar until fluffy.
2. Beat in eggs; add flour and baking powder.
3. Mix in rum. Set batter aside.
4. In a small saucepan, melt butter; add brown sugar, flour and raisins, mixing well.
5. Pour ½ of the batter into a greased round 8" (20 cm) pan. Add raisin filling, reserving ¼ of it.
6. Add remaining batter; sprinkle the top of the batter with reserved filling.
7. Bake at 350°F (180°C) for 50-60 minutes.

Ginger Butter Cake

A dense shortbread-like cake with a rich ginger flavour. Serve it with one of the tropical fresh fruit salads.

2 cups	flour	500 mL
1 cup	sugar	250 mL
¼ tsp.	salt	1 mL
1 cup	chilled unsalted butter	250 mL
¾ cup	finely chopped candied ginger in heavy syrup	175 mL
1 tbsp.	almond extract	15 mL
1	egg, beaten	1

1. In a large bowl, combine the flour, sugar and salt. Cut in the chilled butter with a pastry cutter or 2 knives.
2. Drain the ginger. With a wooden spoon, stir ½ cup (125 mL) of chopped ginger into the batter. Stir in the almond extract and beaten egg. The dough will be very stiff; you may have to knead it with your hands until it holds together. Add 2-3 tbsp. (30-45 mL) of the ginger syrup if you want a more moist cake.
3. Press the dough into an 8" (20 cm) greased round cake pan. Mark the cake into small wedges with a knife. Brush 2 tbsp. (30 mL) of the ginger syrup over the cake and sprinkle with the remaining ¼ cup (60 mL) of chopped ginger.
4. Bake at 350°F (180°C) for 30 minutes, or until golden brown.

It too hat fe hold.

It is too hot to hold.

"Chinese Cakes"

Chinese red bean cakes are traditional, but in the Caribbean they also make black bean cakes. Layering the two types of dough creates a flaky pastry.

BLACK-EYED PEA FILLING:

1 cup	black-eyed peas	250 mL
4 tbsp.	vegetable oil	60 mL
½ cup	sugar	125 mL

FIRST DOUGH:

1 cup	flour	250 mL
4 tbsp.	vegetable oil	60 mL
4 tbsp.	sugar	60 mL

SECOND DOUGH:

1 cup	flour	250 mL
¼ cup	butter OR margarine	60 mL
1	egg, beaten	1

1. Boil black-eyed peas until soft. Sift through a fine sieve. Strain through a muslin cloth to obtain a black-eyed pea paste.
2. In a skillet, heat oil and fry black-eyed pea paste in oil, adding sugar. Cook for about 20 minutes, until the paste leaves the side of the pan and is a jam-like consistency. Let cool.
3. To make the First Dough, in a small bowl, mix the flour, oil and sugar together with a little water to make a bread dough.
4. To make the Second Dough, in a small bowl, mix the flour and butter together. Do not add water.
5. **To assemble the cakes**; divide each batch of dough into 15 pieces.
6. Place a piece of the first dough on a board or in your hand; place a piece of the second dough on top of it. Roll or press the 2 doughs together to form a 6" (15 cm) circle. Fold circle edges into the centre to form a 4" (10 cm) square.
7. Roll out each piece again and fill with black-eyed pea paste. Bring dough edges together to form a flattened ball. Seal edges. Repeat with all 15 cakes.
8. Baste cakes with beaten egg and bake at 350°F (180°C) for 10-15 minutes.

Fruit Cake – Guyana Style

This dark moist cake is filled with fruit and rum.

1 lb.	raisins	500 g
½ lb.	currants	250 g
¼ lb.	prunes	125 g
1 cup	rum	250 mL
1½ lbs.	soft brown sugar (3⅜ cups [800 mL])	750 g
½ cup	hot water	125 mL
½ lb.	butter (1 cup [250 mL])	250 g
6	eggs, beaten	6
1 tsp.	vanilla	5 mL
½ lb.	flour (2 cups [500 mL])	250 g
1 tsp.	baking powder	5 mL
1 tsp	mixed spice (allspice)	5 mL
¼ lb.	mixed peel	125 g
¼ lb.	chopped nuts (optional)	125 g
½ cup	cherry brandy	125 mL

1. Wash and dry fruits. Grind the fruit and soak with ¾ cup (175 mL) of rum. Store, covered, in a glass jar to steep for 3 weeks or longer.
2. To make caramel, heat 1 lb./2¼ cups (500 g/560 mL) of brown sugar until melted; add hot water gradually and simmer until dark brown. Let cool.
3. Cream butter and ½ lb./1⅛ cups (228 g/265 mL) brown sugar well; add beaten eggs a little at a time; add vanilla and rum-soaked fruits, stirring well. Add enough caramel to make the batter as dark as desired.
4. Add sifted flour with baking powder and mixed spice. Fold in peel and chopped nuts.
5. Pour the batter into a 9" (23 cm) springform pan, greased and lined with waxed paper. Bake at 300°F (150°C) for about 2-2½ hours.
6. Pour additional rum and the cherry brandy over the cake immediately after it is baked. Repeat 3 or 4 times. Allow cake to remain in pan until cool.
7. Wrap cooled cake well and store in a cool place in an air-tight container. Cake will keep for several weeks.

Dundee Fruit Cake

This light fruit cake came to the Caribbean with Scottish settlers.

1 cup	butter	250 mL
1 cup	sugar	250 mL
4	eggs	4
1½ cups	flour	325 mL
2 tsp.	baking powder	10 mL
½ tsp.	salt	2 mL
1 tbsp.	milk	15 mL
1 cup	raisins	250 mL
1 cup	currants	250 mL
⅓ cup	mixed peel	75 mL
⅓ cup	red and green cherries, chopped	75 mL
⅓ cup	chopped walnuts	75 mL
	blanched almonds for decoration	

1. In a large bowl, cream butter and sugar until light. Add eggs 1 at a time, beating well after each addition.
2. Sift flour, baking powder and salt. Fold into egg mixture alternating with milk a little at a time.
3. Coat fruits with 3-4 tbsp. (45-60 mL) flour and fold into the batter with the walnuts.
4. Pour the batter into a greased 1½ x 9" (4 x 23 cm) round pan. Decorate with the almonds. Bake at 325°F (160°C) for about 1 hour.

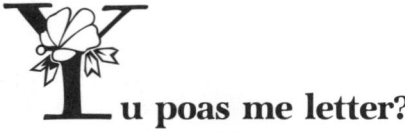

Yu poas me letter?

Did you mail my letter?

Lemon Torte, page 94
Lemon Butter Cream Icing, page 95
Tropical Fruit Punch, page 12
Gulab Jamoon, page 73

Sweet
&
Fruit Breads

Salara – Coconut Roll

*This coconut yeast bread is sweet and tasty, it's also
very decorative, like a strawberry-filled cinnamon roll.*

1 tbsp.	dry yeast	15 mL
¼ cup	warm water	60 mL
¼ cup	sugar	60 mL
1 cup	milk	250 mL
¼ cup	shortening	60 mL
1 tsp.	salt	5 mL
3 cups	flour	750 mL
1	egg, beaten	1
1 tbsp.	butter	15 mL
1	egg white, beaten	1

COCONUT FILLING:

1 cup	grated coconut	250 mL
½ cup	sugar	125 mL
1 tsp.	cinnamon	5 mL
½ tsp.	vanilla	2 mL
5 drops	strawberry food colour	5 drops

1. Dissolve the yeast in warm water. Sprinkle with 1 tsp. (5 mL) of sugar.
   Mix and let stand.
2. Warm the milk. In a large bowl, combine the milk, shortening, salt
   and sugar; add flour and egg. Knead to make a moderately stiff dough.
   Shape dough into a ball.
3. Place dough in a greased bowl and cover; let rise to double the size for
   about 1 hour. Punch down; divide in half. Roll each half into an 8 x
   12" (20 x 30 cm) rectangle. Brush with melted butter.
4. Combine all filling ingredients and let stand for 1 hour.
5. Sprinkle half of the filling mixture on each rectangle of dough. Roll up
   lengthwise; seal edges.
6. Place rolls on a cookie sheet and cover; let rise until double in size.
7. Brush rolls with beaten egg white. Bake at 350°F (180°C) for 20-30
   minutes. Cool before cutting into slices.

Coconut Bread

Coconut bread is popular throughout the Caribbean – there are many versions of this recipe.

4 cups	flour	1 L
2 tsp.	baking powder	10 mL
½ tsp.	salt	2 mL
2 cups	grated fresh OR dessicated coconut	500 mL
¾ cup	sugar	175 mL
1 tsp.	vanilla	5 mL
1	egg, beaten	1
1 cup	milk	250 mL
	sugar	

1. In a large bowl, sift together flour, baking powder and salt. Add coconut, sugar, vanilla and egg. Mix well.
2. Add milk a little at a time until dough is firm but not sticky.
3. Knead for a few minutes. Shape dough into 2 loaves and place into 2 greased 5 x 9" (13 x 23 cm) loaf pans.
4. Dust loaves with sugar and bake at 350°C (180°F) for 1 hour, or until golden brown.

Makes 2 loaves

t bruk.

It is broken.

Cinnamon Raisin Coconut Bread

Delicious, cinnamon and raisins add flavour and texture.

4 cups	flour	1 L
¾ cup	sugar	175 mL
2 tsp.	baking powder	10 mL
½ tsp.	salt	2 mL
1 tsp.	cinnamon	5 mL
1	egg, beaten	1
¾ cup	milk and coconut water	175 mL
¼ lb.	shortening, melted	115 g
1 tsp.	vanilla	5 mL
2 cups	grated coconut	500 mL
4 ozs.	raisins (¾ cup [170 mL]), floured (optional)	115 g
½ cup	sugar for sprinkling	125 mL

1. In a large bowl, combine flour, sugar, baking powder, salt and cinnamon. Add beaten egg, milk, melted shortening and vanilla. Stir in grated coconut and floured raisins, if used.
2. Blend well and pour batter into 2 or 3 greased 5 x 9" (13 x 23 cm) loaf pans, filling about two-thirds full. Sprinkle tops with sugar.
3. Bake at 350°F (180°C), for about 1 hour, until golden brown and centres are dry when pierced with a skewer.

Makes 2 or 3 loaves

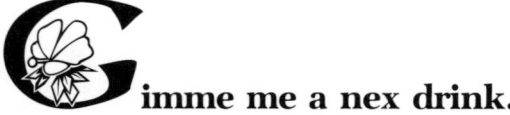

imme me a nex drink.

Give me another drink.

Sweet Coconut-Fruit Bread

Rich with fruit and peel, this coconut bread is lovely for afternoon tea.

³/₄ cup	grated coconut	175 mL
1 cup	sugar	250 mL
1	egg, beaten	1
1 tsp.	vanilla	5 mL
¹/₂ cup	butter OR margarine	125 mL
2 cups	flour	500 mL
2 tsp.	baking powder	10 mL
1 tsp.	allspice	5 mL
³/₄ cup	water OR milk	175 mL
1 cup	raisins	250 mL
¹/₂ cup	maraschino cherries	125 mL
¹/₂ cup	currants	125 mL
¹/₂ cup	mixed peel	125 mL
	sugar and water for glaze	

1. In a large bowl, mix grated coconut with sugar and beaten egg. Add vanilla and butter. Mix thoroughly.
2. Sift dry ingredients and add to coconut mixture.
3. Add just enough water or milk to make a soft dough.
4. Mix in fruits and peel.
5. Pour batter into a greased 5 x 9 (13 x 23 cm) loaf pan and bake at 350°F (180°C) for 50-60 minutes. Remove bread from the oven.
6. Mix a little sugar and water to make a syrup; brush on top of bread. Return bread to the oven for 3-5 minutes.

Makes 1 loaf

Me go show yu weh barley grow.

You will be severely punished.

Pineapple Banana Bread

A moist and tasty blend of pineapple, coconut and banana.

½ cup	butter OR margarine	125 mL
1 cup	sugar	250 mL
3	eggs, beaten	3
1 tbsp.	grated lemon peel	15 mL
½ cup	mashed banana	125 mL
2 cups	flour	500 mL
2 tsp.	baking powder	10 mL
¼ tsp.	salt	1 mL
1 cup	drained crushed pineapple	250 mL
½ cup	dessicated coconut	125 mL

1. In a large bowl, using an electric mixer, cream butter and sugar; add beaten eggs and lemon peel.
2. Mix in mashed bananas.
3. Sift flour, baking powder and salt; add to batter.
4. Fold in pineapple and coconut.
5. Pour batter into a greased 5 x 9" (13 x 23 cm) loaf pan and bake at 350°F (180°C) for 1 hour.

Makes 1 loaf

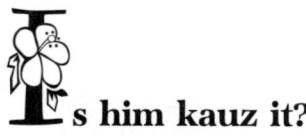

Is him kauz it?

It's his fault.

Mango Nut Bread

Mango sauce makes this bread moist and flavourful.

MANGO SAUCE:

2	ripe mangoes	2
¼ cup	water	60 mL
2 tsp.	lemon juice	10 mL
2 cups	flour	500 mL
1 cup	sugar	250 mL
2 tsp.	baking powder	10 mL
½ tsp.	baking soda	2 mL
½ tsp.	salt	2 mL
¼ tsp.	cinnamon	1 mL
1 cup	chopped walnuts	250 mL
2	eggs, beaten	2
2 tbsp.	melted butter	30 mL

1. To make the sauce, peel mangoes; slice into small pieces and cook with water until softened. Remove from heat.
2. Purée mango pulp in a blender, adding lemon juice.
3. In a medium bowl, sift flour; add sugar, baking powder, baking soda, salt, cinnamon and nuts.
4. In a large bowl, using an electric mixer, combine eggs, butter and 1 cup (250 mL) of mango sauce. Add flour mixture until blended.
5. Pour batter into a greased 5 x 9" (13 x 23 cm) loaf pan and bake at 350°F (180°C) for 1 hour. Cool before slicing.

Makes 1 loaf

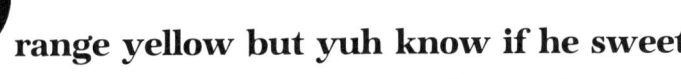

range yellow but yuh know if he sweet.

You can't judge everything from the outside.

Banana Nut Bread

Peanuts or almonds make this banana bread recipe unique.

2 cups	flour	500 mL
1 tbsp.	baking powder	15 mL
¹⁄₂ tsp.	salt	2 mL
¹⁄₂ tsp.	nutmeg	2 mL
¹⁄₂ cup	chopped nuts (peanuts OR almonds)	125 mL
¹⁄₂ cup	butter	125 mL
1 cup	sugar	250 mL
1	egg, beaten	1
3	ripe bananas, mashed	3
¹⁄₂ cup	milk	125 mL
1 tsp.	vanilla	5 mL

1. In a medium bowl, sift together flour, baking powder, salt and nutmeg. Stir in nuts.
2. In a large bowl, using an electric mixer, cream together butter and sugar until light; add beaten egg and mashed bananas. Mix well.
3. Add flour mixture gradually to creamed mixture, alternating with milk and vanilla.
4. Pour batter into a greased 5 x 9" (13 x 23 cm) loaf pan and bake at 350°F (180°C) for 1 hour.
5. The bread is done when a tester inserted in the centre comes out clean. Cool before slicing.

Makes 1 loaf

Don't tie bundle with dem people.

Those people are very unreliable.

Orange Date Bread

Sweet mellow dates and tangy orange peel – a great flavour duo.

¼ cup	butter	60 mL
1 cup	sugar	250 mL
1	egg	1
2 cups	flour	500 mL
1 tsp.	baking powder	5 mL
1 tsp.	baking soda	5 mL
1 cup	warm water	250 mL
2 tbsp.	orange juice	30 mL
1 cup	chopped dates	250 mL
½ cup	chopped nuts	125 mL
1 tbsp.	grated orange peel	15 mL

1. In a large bowl, using an electric mixer, cream butter and sugar. Add egg and beat well.
2. In a small bowl, sift flour, baking powder and baking soda.
3. To the egg mixture, add part of the flour mixture, alternating with the water and orange juice, ending with the flour mixture.
4. Stir in the dates, nuts and orange peel.
5. Pour batter into a greased 5 x 9" (13 x 23 cm) loaf pan and bake at 350°C (180°F) for 1 hour. Cool before slicing.

Makes 1 loaf

Who Gad bless no man cuss.

I'm all right, don't envy (or pity) me.

Zucchini Bread

Zucchini bread is even popular in the Caribbean!

2 cups	flour	500 mL
1 cup	sugar	250 mL
³/₄ cup	chopped walnuts	175 mL
1 tbsp.	baking powder	15 mL
¹/₂ tsp	salt	2 mL
3	eggs	3
¹/₂ cup	vegetable oil	125 mL
1¹/₂ cups	grated zucchini	375 mL
1 tsp.	grated lemon peel	5 mL

1. In a medium bowl, combine flour, sugar, nuts, baking powder and salt.
2. In a large bowl, using an electric mixer, beat eggs; stir in oil, zucchini and lemon peel. Gradually add flour mixture. Combine well.
3. Pour batter into 2 greased 5 x 9" (12 x 23 cm) loaf pans and bake at 350°F (180°C) for 1 hour. Cool bread in pans for at least 10 minutes, before removing.

Makes 2 loaves

Nah mind how pumpkin vine run, he must dry up one day.

Every life comes to an end sooner or later.

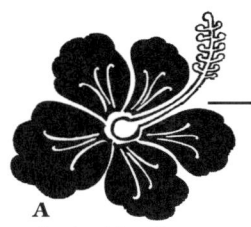

Index

Caribbean Cuisine
by Dr. Betty "K"

Caribbean Cuisine contains traditional favourites from many islands. these recipes retain the exotic flavours of the islands and take you on an international tour of many cultures. They are also adapted to the busy lifestyle of the author and North American cooks. Fabulous appetizers and drinks, soups, salads, breads and desserts will bring island warmth and sunshine into your kitchen. The recipes in *Caribbean Cuisine* are easy to prepare and they adapt beautifully to both special occasion entertaining and family meals. Enjoy this taste of the Caribbean!

Retail $12.95   6" x 9"
120 pages   6 colored photographs
ISBN 1-919845-77-0   perfect bound

Vegetarian Cuisine
by Dr. Betty "K"

These international vegetarian recipes, developed by the physician author of the best-selling *Caribbean Cuisine*, are healthy, appetizing and flavourful additions to any menu. Drawing on her rich Caribbean culinary history, which includes the foods of Europe, Africa, China, India, North and South America, she presents nutritious, high-fibre, low-cholesterol dishes with superb flavour. Nutritional analysis is provided for all recipes.

Retail $12.95   6" x 9"
120 pages   6 colored photographs
ISBN 1-895292-18-2   perfect bound

Send a *Caribbean Treat* to a friend

Caribbean Desserts, Caribbean Cuisine and *Vegetarian Cuisine* are $12.95 per book plus $3.50 (total order) for shipping and handling.

Caribbean Desserts _____ x $12.95 = $ _____

Caribbean Cuisine _____ x $12.95 = $ _____

Vegetarian Cuisine _____ x $12.95 = $ _____

Postage and handling _____ = $ _____ 3.50

Subtotal _____ = $ _____

In Canada add 7% GST OR 15% HST where applicable _____ = $ _____

Total enclosed _____ = $ _____

U.S. and international orders payable in U.S. funds./ Price is subject to change.

NAME: _____

STREET: _____

CITY: _____ PROV./STATE _____

COUNTRY _____ POSTAL CODE/ZIP _____

Please make cheque or money order payable

FAX: 416-283-9285
E-mail: bettyk@idirect.com

For fund raising or volume purchase
for volume rates.   Please a

Mrs Betty Signh
212-228 Bonis Ave
Toronto ON M1T 3W4

Send a *Caribbean Treat* to a friend

Caribbean Desserts, Caribbean Cuisine and *Vegetarian Cuisine* are $12.95 per book plus $3.50 (total order) for shipping and handling.

Caribbean Desserts _____ x $12.95 = $ _____

Caribbean Cuisine _____ x $12.95 = $ _____

Vegetarian Cuisine _____ x $12.95 = $ _____

Postage and handling _____ = $ _____ 3.50

Subtotal _____ = $ _____

In Canada add 7% GST OR 15% HST where applicable _____ = $ _____

Total enclosed _____ = $ _____

U.S. and international orders payable in U.S. funds./ Price is subject to change.

NAME: _____

STREET: _____

CITY: _____ PROV./STATE _____

COUNTRY _____ POSTAL CODE/ZIP _____

Please make cheque or money order payable t

FAX: 416-283-9285
E-mail: bettyk@idirect.com

For fund raising or volume purchases,
for volume rates.   Please allo

Mrs Betty Signh
212-228 Bonis Ave
Toronto ON M1T 3W4